Tax-Effective Charitable Giving

First edition

by
Andrew Burgess

publishing

Tottel Publishing   Maxwelton House, 41–43 Boltro Road, Haywards Heath, West Sussex, RH16 1BJ

A CIP Catalogue record for this book is available from the British Library.

ISBN 1–84592–012–0

Typeset by Phoenix Photosetting, Chatham, Kent

Printed and bound by Hobbs the Printers, Totton, Hampshire

Contents

Contents

Contents

Contents

Table of Cases

Table of Statutes

References at the right-hand side of the column are to paragraph number. Where a paragraph number is in **bold** this indicates that the Act is set out in part or in full.

Table of Statutory Instruments

References at the right-hand side of the column are to paragraph number. Where a paragraph number is in **bold** this indicates that the Statutory Instrument is set out in part or in full.

Chapter 1   Introduction

Background

1.1   The author has been writing books about tax and charities for the past 19 years since he first became involved in writing *Tolley's Charities Manual*. During that time he has written many thousands of words on the subject, and has recorded the details of the many changes in the tax and regulatory regime that have happened to UK charities in the last two decades. There is no doubt that those changes have been significant and have always been promoted as being aimed at positively encouraging charitable giving. So why is it that the same comments are still being made today about the relative lack of charitable giving in the UK and, in particular, the constant reference to our performance as compared to that in the USA?

Start off with some statistics

1.2   Statistics in this area are not easy to come across for some reason. We know that there are something in excess of 175,000 registered charities in the UK and there are many more, such as local church fellowships, that, under current legislation do not have to be registered. That means that a large number of organisations are chasing the finite pot of the wealth of the people. The problem is that charities obtain their funds from many sources and in many diverse ways and it is not always possible to identify sources and amounts to provide accurate statistics.

Two significant charitable organisations – the Charities Aid Foundation (CAF) and the National Council for Voluntary Organisations (NCVO) have tried to put some measure on the level of giving. These organisations published details in August 2003 of analysis of giving to charity in 2002 and their findings can be summarised as follows:

- the total amount given to charities by UK individuals in 2002 was £7.3 billion, up from £6.9 billion in 2001;

- the proportion of people giving to charity remains relatively stable at 67.3%, down slightly from 68.5% in 2001;

- the average monthly donation in 2002 was £12.93, a 4% increase (in real terms) since 2001;

- women gave more than men. The average monthly donation by women was £13.57, well over £1 more than men. Women were also more likely to give in the first place;

- a small group of donors (7.6%) gave more than £50 a month. Although few in number, this group contributed over 60% of the total amount donated;

1

1.3   Introduction

- planned giving has grown – in 2002, 15.3% of donations came from direct debit and standing orders compared with 12.6% in 2001;

- street collections and door-to-door collections remain the most popular ways of giving to charity;

- as in previous years, the two causes that draw the widest support from the general public are medical research (24.1%) and children or young people (20.5%);

- in 2001/02, £1.98 billion was made through Gift Aid and £73m through payroll giving which is the fastest growing method of tax-efficient giving (grown by 33%).

Add in some political comment

1.3   On 26 May 2004, the House of Lords had a debate on an issue raised by Lord Joffe on the fact that individual giving in the UK had fallen from 1.2% of Gross Domestic Product (GDP) in 1992 to 0.9% in 2002, a fall of 25%. The debate gave opportunity for a number of their Lordships, many with connections in the charity world, to impart their observations and ideas on why there was a problem and what could be done to resolve it. A selection of the comments give a flavour of the debate and highlight the issues relating to tax-efficient giving, which are the theme of this book.

Lord Joffe, commenting on the trend shown by the statistics:

> The trend period upon which I will focus runs from 1992 to 2002, the most recent year for which statistics are available. During that period, personal incomes have risen in real terms on average by more than 25 per cent; personal wealth has more than doubled; the Chancellor of the Exchequer, Gordon Brown, has introduced a range of very attractive tax benefits with the objective of stimulating giving; the charitable sector has become much more professional in fundraising; and the very wealthy have prospered as never before. With all those positives, one would have expected the level of individual giving as a percentage of GDP to have increased dramatically.

Trying to find reasons, Lord Joffe continues:

> In seeking to explore the reasons why the level of giving has not risen in line with the growth of incomes, it emerges that the poor who give to charity give on average three times as much as a proportion of their income as the better off, the top 20 per cent of whom give on average only 0.7 per cent. So, we find that the poor, who cannot really afford it, are considerably more generous than the well-off, who can. This is even more astonishing when regard is paid to the statistics that show that the wealthiest 1 per cent of the population own close to one-quarter of the total marketable wealth, while the poorest half of the population own between them only 5 per cent. It follows from those statistics that if the level of giving is to increase significantly, that increase must largely come from the well-off substantially increasing the level of their giving. Unless the very wealthy set an example, it is unlikely that this increase will happen.

He goes on to analyse the *Sunday Times* Rich List and their list of donors, and then turns to where he thinks responsibility lies:

[Charities] must face up to the challenge of proving to donors that they are making a real and positive difference to society; that they are efficient and effective; and that they appreciate and value the support of those who contribute to their work. Having accepted this responsibility, charities must tailor the level of their 'ask' to the income and wealth of the donor, and not be frightened to ask for generous donations from those who can afford them. Increasingly, charities should take potentially generous donors out to show them their work so that such donors gain an understanding of what it is like to live in poverty, or to be without shelter or food, or dying of AIDS. When the wealthy have seen such suffering and realised that they can make a difference, I believe they will want to give generously.

Baroness Pitkeathly, on her last day as chair of the New Opportunities Fund, the largest of the National Lottery distributors, commenting on the influence of the Lottery:

Let us be clear – people do not play the lottery to give money to charity. They play because they think they may win. However, what the 28 pence in the pound that goes to good causes represents to them is a consolation for not winning. It is difficult to over-emphasise what that consolation has done for individuals and communities in the United Kingdom over the past ten years. That £15 billion has a made a huge difference to every community in our country.

Then commenting on the giving of time:

In the view of Volunteering England, willingness to make charitable contributions is alive, well and living here, not only in terms of money but – even more important – in terms of time. A huge amount of time is donated to communities every week. Recent surveys suggest that between 39 per cent and 48 per cent of the adult population volunteer their time through an organisation.

Lord Brooke commenting on one of the cultural issues – the rise of modernisation:

… which is exemplified in the fact that it is the strong brands in the large charities which are at a relative advantage in attracting growing donations. The latter is a function of more professional fundraising, but that has a genuine read across to the world of traditionalist giving.

Lord Phillips of Sudbury, a well-known figure in the legal world as a charity specialist, had strong words to say about the cultural background:

Until we do something about the prevailing culture and restore to it a measure of the sense of value and purpose which, without being too nostalgic, did exist to a greater degree in the past, I do not think that much can be done to increase giving by the rich. Ultimately, charity is about caritas, the word for love, and it is about feeling and heart; it is not about tax breaks or mechanistic considerations.

1.3 Introduction

Lord Moser provided comment about the role of the corporate sector:

> ... at the moment, three per cent of all charity income comes from the corporate sector. That is not a high figure. There is room for serious advance in this field. We should accept that giving by the corporate sector is not necessarily stimulated by the highest charitable thinking; it may be more a matter of competitiveness, corporate image or marketing. I find nothing wrong with that. I am happy as long as firms give to charities and get involved. There is real room for major advance in the corporate sector.

He also put the issue of corporate giving into perspective:

> Some shareholders would cut up rough if their distributed profits were reduced. On the other hand, some companies – I will not begin to mention names – are very active in giving and get away with it happily. The answer surely is that it must become a matter of serious corporate pride. It already is for a number of companies. It is often written about as something about which a company should be proud – about getting involved in the local community and so forth.

Lord Haskel, president of the Institute for Jewish Policy Research, had comments about the role of giving in religious communities and also on giving by the young:

> The research also discovered that young people today are less generous than older people. Perhaps that is in general because they are more secular and believe that the State should provide more support; or perhaps it is because we have the wealthiest generation ever of over-50s, and they can give more. We found the same pattern repeated in volunteering: the older and the more religious do more of it.

> The research seemed to show that giving is also linked to involvement and governance. There is no doubt that the increasing regulation, bureaucracy and legal responsibilities all act as disincentives to involvement.

> We learned that family tradition plays an important part in a culture of giving. In some families there is a strong sense of obligation. Once that chain is broken, it is difficult to rebuild. That is why starting people early and educating them in the importance of charitable giving needs to be emphasised.

Lord Judd perhaps identified the key to giving and pointed out that everything modern is not necessarily best:

> At the heart of it there has to be the passionate conviction of those involved.

> There are dangers in all the new management-speak and the new impersonal mass fund-raising techniques, which frankly fool very few when they are dressed up as personal by the new IT systems available. The concept of a donor basis is hazardous terminology. Fundraising is not primarily about money; sustained and successful fundraising is about relating to individuals and winning their commitment and trust. Identification, involvement and stakeholding matter.

Baroness Noakes, put tax-efficient giving in its place:

> It has for a long time been possible to give money to charities tax-efficiently and the Government's gift aid schemes and other innovations have made that easier. But even so, in 2001–02 tax-efficient giving amounted to less than 30 per cent of the total and so there must be more that could be done to promote tax-efficient schemes. In that context, it is a source of regret that the Treasury sees it as its mission to track down and destroy schemes that they say abuse gift aid, such as the entrance fee arrangements.

Lord McIntosh, summing up for the Government outlined what had been done and put it into perspective:

> We have removed the £250 minimum donation for Gift Aid and simplified the procedures which mean that there has been an increase in gross donations from individuals, including deeds of covenant, from £1.8 billion in 2000–01 to £2.3 billion in 2002–03. We have removed the £1,200 annual ceiling on donations using payroll giving and introduced a three year 10 per cent supplement on donations. That has resulted in an increase in giving from £37 million in 1999–2000 to £86 million in 2002–03. That is very low. The noble Lord, Lord Joffe, gave the figures for payroll giving: 2 per cent in this country and 32 per cent in the United States. It is still very low, but the incentives are there. There is tax relief for gifts of shares, securities and real property to charity.

What is the result?

1.4 The end of this debate was a little inconclusive – it was one of the airing of issues that the House of Lords is able to indulge in – but nothing emerges in concrete proposals. How might we sum it up? Three basic conclusions are drawn up:

- most people are prepared to give something to charity, but those who are committed to a project or ideal will always be most generous;

- charity fundraising organisation can be counter-productive. Modern methods, such as telephone canvassing etc, may not actually be adding anything significant to the overall yield;

- tax incentives enhance what is already being given but are still not providing the incentive to new giving.

This book is not about techniques of fundraising. There are many publications on that subject, and there are many people involved in the fundraising 'industry' who will believe that modern methods do work and that the profession of fundraising has an important role to play in increasing the level of charitable giving in this country. The author would certainly accept that in the effort to compete with non-charitable calls on individual's limited resources, charities need to be seen to behave in a professional way. Charity events need to be organised in the best way possible within available resources. Charities are also competing with each other and here the issue of association with, and commitment to, a cause will outweigh, in the author's view, gimmicks and other tools that might be used.

This book is about tax-efficient fundraising but how do we define that?

What is tax-efficient fundraising?

Two sides to the issue

1.5   There are two sides to this definition – the charity and the donor. The perfect tax efficiency will be that which means that a donation is not going to give the charity a tax problem and, even better, gives it some additional funds, and will give the donor some kind of tax relief. The table below sets out the main types of giving to charity which will be looked at in detail in the later chapters of this book, and identifies the tax position of charity and donor. The table (and, indeed, the book) does not cover the areas of fundraising that are more relevant to the issues of trading. Those types of fundraising, such as events, shops and publications etc, usually involve an element of earning rather than giving, although there may be some element of giving involved, eg paying additional sums for tickets. The background to these areas and the tax issues they raise are discussed in detail in *Tolley's Charity Trading*.

Table 1.1: tax efficiency of different types of giving

Type of giving	*Charity tax position*	*Donor tax position*
Collecting boxes	Not taxable.	No tax relief.
Donated goods	Not taxable.	No tax relief.
Gift Aid	Not taxable. Charity recovers basic-rate tax 'paid' by donor.	Basic-rate tax relief on making donation. Higher-rate tax relief if appropriate. CT relief for corporate donor.
House-to-house collections	Not taxable. May be able to recover basic-rate tax relief if donation is under Gift Aid.	No tax relief unless uses Gift Aid.
Gift of land	Not taxable.	Income tax relief at donor's top rate on value of donation.
Gift of shares	Not taxable.	Income tax relief at donor's top rate on value of donation.
Legacies	Not taxable.	Exempt for IHT.

Payroll giving	Not taxable. Receives gross gift.	Full income tax relief on gross donation.
Stock items from business	Not taxable.	No tax charge on transfer. Cost of production allowed.
Secondment of staff	Not taxable.	Full costs of staff allowed against profits.
Sponsored events	Not taxable. May be able to recover basic-rate tax relief if donation is under Gift Aid.	No tax relief unless uses Gift Aid.
Sponsorship	Usually not taxable (but watch where a trade receipt).	Usually allowable.
Street collections	Not taxable.	No tax relief.
Voluntary donations, eg church collections	Not taxable. May be able to recover basic-rate tax relief if donation is under Gift Aid.	No tax relief unless uses Gift Aid.

The table reflects the position of tax-efficient giving in 2004. The author produced a similar table for a booklet back in the late 1990s, before the major Charity Tax Review was undertaken by the Labour Government, and that table looked very different. The Gift Aid option existed, but there was a minimum donation of £250 required to trigger the relief and so the option of using Gift Aid for things like house-to-house collections and sponsored events was not really viable. The relief for gifts of land and shares did not exist. The limit for payroll giving was set at £1,200 pa so there was no incentive for highly-paid individuals to make significant donations using this route. The routes for business gifts were also limited. Much has changed in a few years and the opportunities are there if charities choose to use them.

Not an open chequebook

1.6 Whilst the Government has been generous in extending the reliefs that it has, the position is still not ideal for charities. VAT remains a major cost for many charities and, despite intense pressure for significant change, the Government remains set against it. The other issue is that the reliefs come at a cost of compliance. This is right because without some measure of control there would be widespread abuse of the system. The tax-avoidance industry is very quick to spot routes to save wealthy individuals and companies large amounts of tax and the use of tax-free vehicles like charities is manna from heaven. Back in the days of high-tax rates in the 1970s and early 1980s when the avoidance industry really boomed, the use of charitable trusts was one of the routes used for tax avoidance. The opportunities are still taken today. The *Finance Act 2004* contains measures designed to block an advantage that some were taking of the relief for gifts of shares. By dint of using various devices, schemes had been devised that effectively gave the 'donor' relief on the full value of the shares being donated but left the value effectively back with the donor and gave the charity very little.

The end result of this is that charities are left to work through a large amount of procedural and accounting controls which add to costs and effort. This is particularly true of the Gift Aid regime where the need for an audit trail and the rules on benefits to donors are significant issues. These are covered in **Chapters 2–4**, but charities should also take note of the information in **Chapter 9** which explains how the Inland Revenue police the system and the potential problems that can arise where procedures are not followed properly.

Tax efficiency for individuals and business

1.7   Taxpayers come in many different shapes and sizes; from individuals paying tax at the basic rate through to large corporations paying tax on their mega profits. Tax-efficient giving opportunities are available to both and **Table 1.2** summarises the options they have using the same areas of giving that were considered in **Table 1.1** above.

Table 1.2: Types of giving for individuals and companies

Type of giving	*Individual donors*	*Corporate donors*
Collecting boxes	No tax relief.	Not an option.
Donated goods	No tax relief.	No tax relief.
Gift Aid	Basic-rate tax relief on making donation. Higher-rate tax relief if appropriate.	CT relief provided profit made.
House-to-house collections	No tax relief unless uses Gift Aid.	Not relevant.
Gift of land	Income tax relief at donor's top rate on value of donation.	CT relief on value of donation.
Gift of shares	Income tax relief at donor's top rate on value of donation.	CT relief on value of donation.
Legacies	Exempt for IHT.	Not relevant.
Payroll giving	Full income tax relief on gross donation.	Not relevant other than providing a conduit for employees to donate.
Stock items from business	If a trader. No tax charge on transfer. Cost of production allowed.	No tax charge on transfer. Cost of production allowed.

Secondment of staff	If a trader. Full costs of staff allowed against profits.	Full costs of staff allowed against profits.
Sponsored events	No tax relief unless uses Gift Aid.	No tax relief unless uses Gift Aid.
Sponsorship	If a trader – usually allowable.	Usually allowable.
Street collections	No tax relief.	Not relevant.
Voluntary donations, eg church collections	No tax relief unless uses Gift Aid.	No tax relief unless uses Gift Aid.

The chapters on Gift Aid and giving shares and land will be relevant to companies as well as to individuals – see **Chapters 2–4**. Companies should have an interest in **Chapter 7** on payroll giving because they have an important role in encouraging employees to participate and in providing the opportunity for participation. **Chapter 8** deals specifically with business giving.

A legal framework

The need for regulation

1.8   It is not only the tax area of giving that is subject to regulation; the process of fundraising is now much more closely controlled than ever before. The *Charities Act 1992* and *Charities Act 1993* set out rules that govern the use of professional fundraisers and the links between charities and commercial organisations. The rules on the conduct of street collections and house-to-house collections were also due to be changed, but the necessary regulations have not been pushed through and old regulations currently still apply. A new Charities Bill will see those rules brought on to the statute book together with further regulations to cover the activities of fundraisers who use 'dialoguers' who seek committed giving in the street.

The legal framework is extensive and needs to be understood by charities. A detailed review of the legislation can be found in Mazars & Withers *Tolleys Charities Manual* (LexisNexis). There is comment in this looseleaf in Chapter 9 on the role the Charity Commission will play in the regulation of giving and the issues that can arise when care is not taken.

Chapter 2　Gift Aid – the Charity Perspective

Introduction

2.1　Donations from members of the public and business form a significant proportion of the income of many charities. The donations may take many different forms – church collections, street collections, house-to-house collections, sponsored events of all types, major telethons and appeals in times of special need, such as famine relief. In addition, a number of charities which have a membership rely heavily on subscriptions from their members. In their basic form, donations are not tax efficient – they are not taxable in the charity but they will provide no tax relief to the donor.

For many years, tax efficiency in giving was provided by deeds of covenant. These were legal arrangements entered into by donors to commit themselves to regular giving for a minimum four-year period. The arrangements were cumbersome and charities and donors regularly ran into problems with the Inland Revenue because procedures were not followed or not properly understood.

Gift Aid was originally introduced in 1990 by John Major when he was Chancellor of the Exchequer. The original concept was aimed at providing tax relief where the donation was a one-off and was over £600; this was later reduced to £250. The take up was, therefore, limited and charities still made use of the rather more cumbersome deed of covenant to gain tax benefits on gifts of smaller amounts. The paperwork required by the original Gift Aid was also more onerous, requiring forms to be completed for each gift even when the same taxpayer was involved.

All that changed when, as part of the wide-ranging Charity Tax Review in the late 1990s, the cash limits on Gift Aid were swept away and the paperwork considerably simplified. To call the changes a 'revolution' in charitable giving would not be an understatement. They have transformed the position for many charities that are reliant on donor funds and other direct fundraising as distinct from being dependent upon grants or endowments generating income. The big danger is that, in an attempt to maximise the benefits of what is sometimes referred to as 'new' Gift Aid, some charities have taken short cuts in the procedures or have tried to apply Gift Aid in situations where it was not intended to work.

The essence of the new system is one of flexibility. It is designed to cope with donations made in cash, by direct debit, by cheque, by credit card or by debit card. It will cope with donations made by handing over money in the church collection, by sending money through the post, making a credit card donation over the telephone or over the Internet. It will cope with one-off donations, donations to be made over a specified period of time or all donations to be made to the same charity for the lifetime of the donor. In every case, if the basic conditions are complied with, the charity will be able to uplift the sum received by a tax reclaim from the Government.

2.2 Gift Aid – the Charity Perspective

The importance of Gift Aid in the fundraising armoury of the charity is highlighted by the fact that three chapters are devoted to it in this book. This chapter looks at the issue from the point of view of the charity, and will explain the legal framework within which Gift Aid operates for charities, the administrative arrangements that need to be in place and the all-important accounting issues which go to make up the audit trail. **Chapter 3** will look at the arrangements from the point of view of the donor – how individuals and companies can obtain their tax relief. An understanding of these issues is important for charities so that they can look at ways of increasing their income from Gift Aid by stressing the donor advantages, but also so that they can avoid some donors falling into tax difficulties. **Chapter 4** looks at an important issue that provides a limiting factor on excessive use of Gift Aid – the question of benefit being provided for the donor. This is not a new issue post-2000 – it was part of the original 1990 legislation – but was little understood because Gift Aid had only a limited interest. In the era of no-limit Gift Aid, it assumes an importance which charities will ignore at their peril.

Legal background

Legal conditions

2.2 The basis of Gift Aid was set out in the enabling legislation introduced in 1990. *Finance Act 1990, s 25* is the source legislation, although that section was significantly amended by the *Finance Act 2000*. It is important that charities understand fully the legal basis on which Gift Aid operates.

A payment under Gift Aid is to be referred to as a 'qualifying donation' and must satisfy certain specified conditions. Those conditions (*Finance Act 1990, s 25(2)*) are:

- it takes the form of a payment of a sum of money;

- it is not subject to a condition as to repayment;

- it does not constitute a sum falling within the payroll deduction scheme;

- neither the donor nor any person connected with him receives a benefit in consequence of making it exceeding specified limits;

- it is not conditional on, or associated with, or part of an arrangement involving, the acquisition of property by the charity, otherwise than by way of gift from the donor or a person connected with him; and

- the donor is resident in the UK, or performs duties of an employment which would be treated as performed in the UK or, if non-resident, has UK income or gains liable to tax in the UK.

The conditions relating to benefit will be considered in detail in **Chapter 4**, and those relating to residency will be covered in **Chapter 3**.

Payment

2.3   The Gift Aid provisions can be applied only to payments. The Inland Revenue takes this as meaning cash payments, with cash including cheque and credit card payments. Transfers of assets to a charity or donations in kind will not qualify. Nor, according to the Inland Revenue, is it possible to simply write off a loan. This view was challenged at the Special Commissioners in *Battle Baptist Church v IRC and Woodham [1995] STC (SCD) 176.* The author attended the hearing in January 1995. The decision says very little about the point at issue. The author is grateful to the church for allowing the chapter to describe a fuller version of events. The case serves to show that charities should be prepared to stand and fight against the Inland Revenue in worthwhile situations.

Unfortunately, the decision in the case turned on a technicality, and the Special Commissioner did not make any specific comment on what had been seen as the definitive issue – whether a loan write-off could be regarded as a payment. The Inland Revenue will still maintain its view that there has to be a cash payment, but the background facts do not necessarily fully support that view.

BATTLE BAPTIST CHURCH CASE

2.4   The facts of the case were very simple – the church had received several loans, and after the introduction of Gift Aid, two lenders wrote to the church forgiving their loans. The terms of the release were as follows:

> Please would you cancel the loan … and accept the (amount) as a gift to the building fund.

The church treated these sums as payments under Gift Aid and received repayment from the Inland Revenue. The matter was queried by the Inland Revenue on a subsequent inspection. In the course of subsequent correspondence, the Inland Revenue maintained that the payments did not represent a payment of a sum of money. The Inland Revenue went as far as to say to the church that it could not now pay the money back to the lenders and receive sums back in cash which would qualify for Gift Aid.

At the hearing, the Special Commissioner questioned whether a loan could actually be released by a simple letter, or whether it required a formal deed. The Inland Revenue solicitor took this point and the Commissioner allowed an adjournment for the church to take advice, since this was the first time the Inland Revenue had raised this point. Having taken advice, the church did not feel that it was right to proceed, and the case has now been lost on that point.

The Special Commissioner's decision is very critical of the Inland Revenue for not having raised the issue of the need for a deed, and he comments that the written advice that no repayment could be made 'positively obscured' the position. He comments that:

> … it is unfortunate that time and trouble should have been expanded unnecessarily in preparing these appeals …

2.5   Gift Aid – the Charity Perspective

Where did this decision leave matters? If the legal position was that the loans had not been released, then they still existed. The church was able to actually repay the loans, and the lenders were then able to re-donate the money, making another Gift Aid claim. Obviously, the loan repayment could not, in any way have been conditional upon the sum being re-donated. That is still the safest way of proceeding if a lender indicates to a charity that they are not seeking repayment of their loan. There is a risk to the charity that the sum will not be re-donated, but this is a risk worth taking.

When the original legislation was introduced in 1990 there was a debate on the proposals in the Standing Committee which considers the Finance Act each year. There was discussion about the phrase, 'takes the form of a payment of a sum of money', but that debate was somewhat confused. What the Government of the day were clear about was that Gift Aid could not be applied to gifts in kind. A member of the Committee said in connection with the phrase:

> I understand that to mean that the gift must be in cash, not in kind, but I hope the Economic Secretary (to the Treasury) will correct me if I am wrong.

That view was confirmed but a subsidiary point about writing-off loans was not properly answered.

BOOKKEEPING ENTRIES

2.5   Another line of argument to be considered is that relating to the bookkeeping entries which are needed in this type of situation. The original receipt of the cash loan would be recorded as a debit to the bank account and a credit to a loan account. The church has received money, but has an equal liability to repay it. When the loan is forgiven, the loan account is debited, and the relevant fund credited. The sum of money remains in the bank account, but is now a gift – not a loan. Does this constitute a payment?

In another situation, where a director is voted a bonus and the sum is credited to his loan account with the company, the Inland Revenue is very keen to argue that such a book entry constitutes a payment for the purposes of the employment tax legislation. Indeed, they have case law backing for this with *Garforth v Newsmith Stainless Ltd [1979] STC 129*. The legislation in *Finance Act 1990, s 25* refers to the gift being in 'the form of a payment', there would seem to be a similarity between the two situations.

FOREIGN CURRENCY

2.6   There is no requirement that the payment must be in sterling. At the start of 2002 on the conversion of many European currencies to the Euro, charities were inviting donors to pass to them unwanted coins, the Inland Revenue confirmed that such donations could be made effective for Gift Aid. The same position applies for charities which encourage donations of unwanted 'holiday' cash. The value of the donation is to be the sterling value of the currency on the day the donation is made.

Conditions

2.7   The legislation only refers to conditions as to repayment; it does not appear to prevent the donor placing conditions on what the charity is to do with the gift. The gift must be an absolute gift – a loan to a charity cannot qualify. Nor would a payment qualify if it was earmarked for some specific purpose with the condition that, if the charity did not proceed with that purpose, the gift should be repaid.

Property purchase

2.8   The requirement that the donation should not be related to a property transaction involving the donor is clearly intended to prevent Gift Aid being used as a means of actually benefiting the donor. Without the restriction (and assuming sufficient income on the part of the donor) it would be possible for a donor to give, say, £45,000 to a charity, the charity would reclaim tax of £12,692 (assuming a 22% basic rate) and could then purchase a property from the donor for, say, £55,000.

It should not be assumed that the word 'property' is limited to 'real estate'; it can cover any kind of property which would include chattels such as trading stock, or intellectual property such as rights over software, or copyright on music or books.

The restriction extends to situations where the purchase of property is from someone connected with the donor. The definition of 'connected person' for these purposes is defined by the *Income and Corporation Taxes Act 1988, s 839.* This defines an individual as being connected with another individual if he or she is a spouse, sibling, ancestor or lineal descendant. It also applies connection to a sibling, ancestor or lineal descendant of their spouse, and to the spouses of any relative of the individual or their spouse.

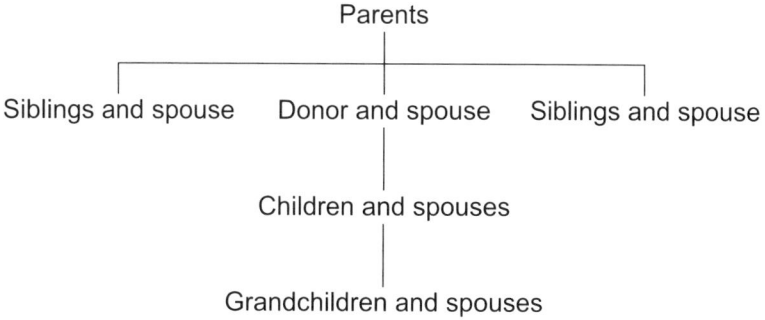

Put in diagrammatic form, 'connection' covers the following.

2.9 Gift Aid – the Charity Perspective

EXAMPLE 2.1

Alex makes a donation to a charity to enable them to purchase a computer from a shop run by Bryan who is married to Claire who is sister of Alex's wife Doreen. There is a connection as defined by the legislation and Gift Aid should not be claimed.

It could be argued that the charity may not know the connection between Alex and Bryan. It is suggested that if a gift is made on condition that a specific source is used to purchase an asset, the charity should make it their business to check out if there is any connection between the donor and the source of the goods.

COMPANY CONNECTIONS

2.9 The connection also extends to companies. An individual is connected with a company if that individual controls that company either on his or her own, or with people who are 'connected' with the individual. So, if in the example above, Bryan traded his business through Bryan Limited in which he and Claire each owned 50% of the shares, then there would be sufficient connection to invalidate the gift.

Companies are also connected with any company they control, or where both companies are controlled by the same people or group of people. This means that care has to be taken where Gift Aid donations are made by a company and there is a request for goods to be purchased from another company in the same group, or what is known as an 'associated' company.

The issue of connection will arise in **Chapter 4** when the question of benefits arising as a result of a donation are considered.

Tax relief for the charity

2.10 Assuming that the conditions are met, then any donation to a charity that meets the requirement of being a 'qualifying donation' will result in the charity being able to reclaim tax from the Inland Revenue. The basis of this claim is that the individual donor has effectively transferred to the charity a sum which is net of basic-rate tax, and since the charity has a tax exemption for this type of income (assuming the funds are applicable and applied for charitable purposes), the charity is entitled to a repayment of the basic rate tax it has suffered.

The amount reclaimable will vary according to both the 'net' donation and the prevailing basic rate of income tax as the following table shows.

Table 2.1: Tax reclaim by charity on Gift Aid

Net payment	Assuming a basic rate of 22%		Calculation based on each 1%	
	Tax reclaimed	Value to charity	Tax reclaimed	Value to charity
1	0.28	1.28	0.01	1.01
10	2.82	12.82	0.10	1.10
50	14.10	64.10	0.50	50.50
100	28.20	128.20	1.00	101.00
250	70.51	320.51	2.52	252.52
500	141.02	641.02	5.05	505.05
1,000	282.05	1,282.05	10.10	1,010.10

A simple formula which calculates the value to a charity of any payment under a deed is:

$$\text{Net payment} \times \frac{100}{100 - \text{basic rate of income tax}}$$

Getting the paperwork right

The new rules in outline

2.11 The removal of the Gift Aid limit opens up all payments to the possibility of being treated as qualifying donations, and many charities must have been concerned at the amount of paperwork that was going to be required. In addition, the Government was keen that donors should be able to make qualifying donations in any way which suited them, including by telephone and the Internet. The system of paperwork had to be flexible if the whole arrangement was not going to drown under a sea of paper, or become so unwieldy for charities to operate that they would simply not do so and thus lose the benefits which the new scheme potentially offered.

The new paperwork is based around what is known as the Gift Aid declaration which has a number of key features as follows:

- the declaration can be in writing or it can be oral with a written record being made;

- it can relate to a specific donation, or a series of donations, or all donations or any arrangement that suits the donor;

- the charity is able to produce its own version although there are Regulations which prescribe certain conditions which must be complied with (the Inland Revenue has produced a model which can be used);

2.12   Gift Aid – the Charity Perspective

- the charity must ensure that it has an audit trail which enables all qualifying donations to be identified in the books from receipt onwards.

REQUIREMENTS

2.12 The rules are not particularly onerous but they must be complied with, and charities will be foolish if they try to take short cuts. The Regulations which set the framework are the *Donations to Charity by Individuals (Appropriate Declarations) Regulations 2000 (SI 2000/2074)*. The Regulations are basically very simple. They set out four basic requirements:

- the key components of a written declaration;
- the key components of an oral declaration;
- the circumstances in which an oral declaration can be nullified;
- the circumstances in which a declaration is cancelled.

The requirements are straightforward and allow considerable flexibility to charities and open up a wide range of situations in which Gift Aid can be used successfully. The key is to follow the basic rules and adapt them carefully to the different sets of circumstances. A few minutes spent checking the paperwork can save many anxious hours later if the Inland Revenue challenges the validity of the declaration, not to mention the possible tax loss if it transpires that the declaration was invalid.

Written declaration

2.13 The written declaration must be used in all circumstances except where the donation is made orally using a credit or debit card over the telephone. The Regulations set out the essential details which must be shown on the written declaration as being:

- the donor's name;
- the donor's address;
- the charity's name or acronym;
- a description of the donations to which the declaration relates;
- a declaration that the donations are to be effective for Gift Aid;
- a note explaining that it is a requirement that the donor must have paid sufficient tax to cover the tax on the donation;
- the date of the declaration.

Note that there is no legal requirement for the declaration to be signed by the donor, but there is nothing to prevent the charity from including this on the declaration if they wish to do so. The Inland Revenue has published some guidance for charities on what they expect to see in the new system and this is considered in more detail in the following paragraphs.

The written declaration can be on plain paper, it can be transmitted by fax, it could be transmitted to the charity as an email attachment or it could be a form already set up on the charity's own website for completion by a donor who is making a donation over the Internet. There is also nothing to prevent an individual preparing his or her own declaration provided that it meets the legal requirements.

THE DONOR'S NAME AND ADDRESS

2.14 This information is essential to the audit trail because the charity must be able to identify who the donor is. The Inland Revenue has to be able to trace the donor through the tax system if necessary, either to check their existence or to verify that the donor has, indeed, paid sufficient tax. The Inland Revenue taxpayer tracing system is now sufficiently accurate to enable it to trace from name and address and it no longer needs a tax reference or National Insurance number to do so.

The Inland Revenue recommendation is that the charity should obtain if possible the title, forenames and surname of the donor. The very least they should obtain are initials and surname. The full postal address, including the postcode should be obtained. If the donor subsequently moves whilst the declaration is still in operation, an incorrect address will not invalidate the declaration, but if a new address is advised, the updated information should be recorded.

THE CHARITY NAME

2.15 The charity must be clearly identifiable using either its full name, or usual name or acronym. The charity could have this pre-printed on the declaration if they wished. There would be nothing to prevent a donation being earmarked for a specific fund, eg High Street Methodist Church Building Fund if that was what the donor wanted provided the name of the charity itself was clearly shown. The donation may then be subject to restrictions as to its use by the charity if the fund concerned was a designated fund.

DESCRIPTION OF THE DONATION

2.16 This is where the greatest care must be taken because there is such a wide scope available. The key point for the charity to remember is that the actual donation should always match the description in the declaration – failure to do this will cause the donation to fall outside the system. The broad possibilities to consider are set out in the table below.

Table 2.2: Wording for Gift Aid declaration

Wording on declaration	What it covers
'the donation I made to you on dd/mm/yy'	This covers the specific donation made on that date and nothing else.
'the enclosed donation'	This might be used on a house-to-house collection envelope. It would relate to that donation only. On a practical level, the charity would need to ensure that when the envelope was opened, the amount was recorded on the envelope and that envelope was retained.
'all donations made under the direct debit mandate below'	This would cover the donations paid under the direct debit and no others. It might be useful for regular donations but it would mean that any other donations made by the same individual would need further declarations.
'all donations made under the standing order of £100 pa signed on dd/mm/yy'	Similar comments as above apply.
'all donations I make from the date of this declaration until dd/mm/yy'	Donations to be made over a fixed period could be covered by wording such as: This declaration would cover every donation made in the specified period in whatever form they were made. Once the period had ended, no further declarations could be included.'
'all donations I make on or after the date of this declaration' or 'all donations I make from this date until further notice'	These are open-ended donations and the declaration will cover all future donations no matter how they are made.
'all donations I make or have made since 6 April 2000'	This is an open-ended declaration that will cover not just future donations but also any made earlier (provided that they can be identified as coming from the donor). The date to be used cannot be earlier than 6 April 2000 when new Gift Aid was introduced. Obviously, if the charity was not in existence at that date, the earliest date will be the establishment of the charity.

The ideal format for ease of administration is clearly the open-ended declaration. All the charity then has to do is to ensure that it can identify all donations coming from that particular donor. There is a danger that these declarations could be overlooked by donors and charities who hold them might want to remind donors periodically that they are holding the declarations. The opportunity could be taken to remind donors of the sums actually paid in each tax year and to check at the same time that the donor remains a taxpayer (or at least is paying sufficient tax to cover the tax on the donations).

Where a donor wished to change the description of the donations to be included, it may be simpler to cancel the first declaration and give the charity a fresh declaration. There are no legal issues involved in this as there were with deeds of covenant because the declaration is not a legally binding obligation to make payments, simply an indication that the donor wishes to have the specified donations treated as qualifying donations.

TREATMENT AS GIFT AID DONATIONS

2.17 The donor must indicate that he or she wishes the donations to be effective for Gift Aid purposes. The Inland Revenue has indicated that charities can use whatever form of words they wish and give the following as examples.

(a) 'Please treat my donations as Gift Aid donations.'

(b) 'I want my donations to be Gift Aid donations.'

(c) 'Please reclaim tax on my donations.'

(d) 'I want the charity to reclaim tax on my donations.'

(e) 'I want the charity to reclaim tax on my donations – yes/no' (delete as appropriate).

(f) 'Tick here if you want us to reclaim tax on your donations.'

The latter two seem to be strange – if someone were to delete 'yes', why were they bothering to make a declaration in the first place? Equally, why would they not want to tick the box? The wording might be appropriate, however, in the context of the written record of an oral declaration which is discussed at **2.20** below.

To avoid any problems, it would appear simplest to use the form of words of either (a) or (b) above. Again these can be pre-printed on the declaration by the charity.

TAXPAYER REQUIREMENT

2.18 The Regulations require that there must be a statement 'explaining the effect of *section 25(8)* of the *Finance Act 1990*'. This is the legal requirement that the donor must have paid sufficient income tax and capital gains tax in the year to cover the tax which will be reclaimed by the charity. As will be seen in **Chapter 3**, a failure to do this could be expensive for the donor and it is right that donors should be warned. The wording could take the form of a warning note on the declaration, for example:

> You must pay an amount of income tax and/or capital gains tax at least equal to the tax that the charity will reclaim on your donations in the tax year (currently 28p for every £1 you give).

The alternative could be to effectively have the donor make a declaration that he or she is a taxpayer. For example, at the start of the declaration include the following:

> I confirm that I am a UK taxpayer, and that the amount of income tax or capital gains tax that I pay in any tax year will cover any tax that the charity may reclaim in respect of my giving.

It might also be helpful to include a reminder to the donor to notify the charity immediately if he or she ceases to be a taxpayer.

HAVING SUPPLIES OF DECLARATIONS AVAILABLE

2.19 Charities who regularly seek donations may want to have a ready supply of declarations available. They do not have to be in pre-printed form, although this would be sensible where, for example, the charity is running a special appeal through local branches or other agencies. Where the charity has facilities for donors to pay in donations at banks, building societies or post offices, it may want to ensure that such locations have stocks of Gift Aid declarations and that local staff in those institutions are encouraged to draw the attention of donors to them.

Charities running sponsored events should ensure that individual participants have a stock of the declarations and that some prominent notice about signing a declaration is included on the sponsor form. The Inland Revenue has produced a standard format for a combined sponsorship and Gift Aid declaration.

Oral declarations

2.20 Where a donor makes a donation by credit card or debit card over the telephone, this can be made into a qualifying donation provided a written record is made and sent to the donor. Charities who are operating this type of fundraising will need to ensure that the people handling the telephone calls are trained in how to maximise the opportunity and to ensure that the paperwork is correct.

The basic information which must be entered on the written record at the time the oral declaration is made is as follows:

- donor's name;
- donor's address;
- charity name or acronym;
- description of the donations;
- declaration that the donations are to be treated as gift aid donations.

In addition, the written record must show:

- a note explaining the requirement with regard to paying tax;
- a note explaining the donor's right to cancel the declaration retrospectively;
- the date on which the donor gave the declaration;
- the date on which the written record is sent to the donor.

In practice, it is likely that the donation details will relate to the specific donation being made over the phone. The Gift Aid treatment can be dealt with by the Yes/No question to be asked by the telephonist. The form can be pre-printed so that the telephonist knows the information to seek over the phone and the record can be despatched as quickly as possible. The charity may want to have a system for checking the written records before they are sent out.

The Regulations do not actually state what should be done with the written record. In practical terms, it must be sent to the donor *and* a copy retained by the charity to provide evidence as part of the audit trail, therefore, the charity must ensure that a copy is taken at some stage. Inland Revenue guidance indicates that the record can be held electronically and transmitted electronically to the donor.

The charity cannot reclaim the tax in respect of an oral declaration until the written record has been sent. Once that has happened a claim can go in, but the charity will have to repay the tax to the Inland Revenue if the donor decides to cancel the declaration.

Cancellation of declarations

2.21   The donor has the right to cancel a declaration at any time, although the effect of the cancellation may differ according to the type of declaration. The notice of cancellation can be made however the donor chooses. It can be made:

- in writing;
- via e-mail;
- in a fax; or
- during a conversation.

In the latter case the charity may want to ensure that a written note is made of the conversation.

Where the declaration was made in writing, the cancellation takes effect from the date on which it is made and will apply to all donations received after that date or from a future date which may be specified by the donor. The latter may happen if the donor knows that in the following tax year they will not be paying sufficient tax to cover the tax on the donations; in that case, the cancellation may be stated to take effect from 6 April next or some such wording. The donor cannot cancel a declaration in respect of a donation already made. If the donor discovers that they have not paid enough tax to cover the donation, it is then too late and he or she must face the consequences as far as that donation is concerned.

Where the donor has made an oral declaration that can be cancelled within 30 days of the date on which the charity sent the written record, the cancellation is retrospective and relates back to the time of the original declaration which, therefore, has no tax effect at all.

Particular types of declaration

2.22   It will normally be assumed that a declaration is going to be made by an individual, but there are two situations in which more than one person may wish to be a party to a declaration.

Spouses or persons living together can make a joint declaration. They must ensure that both names appear on the declaration and it is clear how the donation is to be split between them. The charity will need to identify both parties separately in their records and when making their repayment claim. It follows that both parties must be taxpayers, otherwise some, or all, of the donation will be ineffective.

Where a partnership wishes to make a Gift Aid donation, the situation will depend on where the partnership is located. Partnerships in England, Wales and Northern Ireland are not legal entities and cannot enter directly into a Gift Aid declaration. If the partnership deed, or some other document given under seal, allows one partner to make a declaration on behalf of all partners, that can be done. In that case, the total sum will be divided between the partners in whatever way they choose, but in the event of any indication to the contrary this will be the same as the profit-sharing ratio. Each partner will indicate his or her share of the payment on his or her own tax returns. A partnership in Scotland is a legal entity and could, therefore, enter into its own declaration.

Examples of declarations

2.23   Charities obtain donations in different ways and they will want to have some idea of the type of wording that could be used to meet specific circumstances. The examples that follow cover the following types of donation:

(a)   the Inland Revenue model;

(b)   house-to-house collection;

(c)   sponsored event (this is the Inland Revenue model);

(d)   regular giving to a church;

(e)   membership subscription;

(f)   a credit card donation over the telephone.

Three important caveats must be made:

- with the exception of (a) and (c) above, none have been approved by the Inland Revenue. Inland Revenue approval is not a requirement but clearly it would indicate that there should be no problem;

- the names of the charities used are intended to be fictitious;

- the declarations do not take into account the possibility of benefits being received which may invalidate the donation as a qualifying donation. The conditions relating to benefits are discussed in **Chapter 4**.

Inland Revenue model Gift Aid declaration

Gift Aid declaration

Name of Charity:

Details of donor:
Title: Forename(s):   Surname:
Address:
Postcode:

I want the charity to treat:
* the enclosed donation of £ …
* the donation(s) of £ …which I made on … / … / …
* all donations I make from the date of this declaration until I notify you otherwise
* all donations I have made since 6 April 2000, and all donations I make from the date of this declaration until I notify you otherwise
as Gift Aid donations.
* delete as appropriate

Date … / … / …

Notes:

1. You can cancel this declaration at any time by notifying the charity.

2. You must pay an amount of income tax and/or capital gains tax at least equal to the tax that the charity reclaims on your donations in the tax year (currently 28p for each £1 you give).

3. If, in the future, your circumstances change and you no longer pay tax on your income and capital gains equal to the tax the charity reclaims, you can cancel your declaration (see note 1).

4. If you pay tax at the higher rate you can claim further tax relief in your self-assessment tax return.

5. If you are unsure whether your donations qualify for Gift Aid tax relief, ask the charity or ask your local tax office for leaflet IR113 Gift Aid.

6. Please notify the charity if you change your name or address.

Suggested Gift Aid declaration for house-to-house collection

Gift Aid declaration

Distressed Taxpayers Society

Details of donor:
Title: *Mr*   Forename(s): *Nigel*   Surname: *Brown*
Address: *11 Downandout Street,*
          Littlehampton   Post Code: *PO1 1OR*

I want the charity to treat:
* the enclosed donation of *£1.00* as a Gift Aid donation.

Date: *15/9/04*

Notes:

1. You can cancel this declaration at any time by notifying the charity.

2. You must pay an amount of income tax and/or capital gains tax at least equal to the tax that the charity reclaims on your donations in the tax year (currently 28p for each £1 you give).

3. If you pay tax at the higher rate you can claim further tax relief in your self-assessment tax return.

Note:

In practical terms this declaration will need to be printed on to the collecting envelope.

If the amount of the donation is not shown by the donor, it should be recorded on the envelope by the person who opens it and should be recorded as a personal donation in the cash record.

The envelope should be retained as a prime record.

Inland Revenue model for sponsorship and Gift Aid declaration form

Charity X Sponsorship and Gift Aid Declaration form

We, who have given our names and addresses below, and who have ticked the box entitled '[...] Gift Aid?' want the above charity to reclaim tax on the donation detailed below, given on the date shown. We understand that each of us must pay income tax or capital gains tax equal to the tax reclaimed by the charity on the donation.

Full name	Home address	Postcode	Amount pledged	Amount given	Date given	Gift Aid? [...]

Suggested Gift Aid declaration for regular church giving

Gift Aid declaration

Sunny Street Evangelical Church

Details of donor:
Title: Forename(s):   Surname:
Address:
                                                          Post Code:

I confirm that I am a UK taxpayer and will pay sufficient income tax or capital gains tax to cover the tax being reclaimed by the charity on my donations. I want the charity to treat the payments I make under the direct debit mandate completed below as Gift Aid donations.

Date ... / ... / ...

Direct debit mandate

27

Notes:

1.   You can cancel this declaration at any time by notifying the charity.

2.   If, in the future, your circumstances change and you no longer pay tax on your income and capital gains equal to the tax the charity reclaims you can cancel your declaration (see note 1).

3.   If you pay tax at the higher rate you can claim further tax relief in your self-assessment tax return.

4.   If you are unsure whether your donations qualify for Gift Aid tax relief, ask the charity or ask your local tax office for leaflet IR113 Gift Aid.

5.   Please notify the church if you change your name or address.

Suggested Gift Aid declaration for membership subscription

Gift Aid declaration

Greater Rotherham Organisation of Amateur Numismatists (GROAN)

Details of member:
Title: Forename(s):   Surname:
Address:
                                             Post Code:

I want the charity to treat my annual subscription payable under the attached direct debit mandate as a Gift Aid donation until such time as I cancel my membership.

Date ... / ... / ...

Direct debit mandate

Notes:

1.   You can cancel this declaration at any time by notifying the society.

2.   You must pay an amount of income tax and/or capital gains tax at least equal to the tax that the charity reclaims on your donations in the tax year (currently 28p for each £1 you give).

3. If, in the future, your circumstances change and you no longer pay tax on your income and capital gains equal to the tax the charity reclaims, you can cancel your declaration (see note 1).

4. If you pay tax at the higher rate you can claim further tax relief in your self-assessment tax return.

5. If you are unsure whether your donations qualify for Gift Aid tax relief ask the charity or ask your local tax office for leaflet IR113 Gift Aid.

6. Please notify the society if you change your name or address.

Suggested Gift Aid declaration for a credit card donation

Written record of an oral Gift Aid declaration

African Famine Relief

Details of donor:
Title: Forename(s):   Surname:
Address: Post Code:

I want the charity to treat my donation of £ ... made by telephone on ... / ... / ... as a Gift Aid donation.

Date written record sent to donor ... / ... / ...

Notes:

1. You can cancel this declaration at any time within 30 days of the date this record was sent to you by notifying the charity. If you do so, your donation will not be valid for Gift Aid purposes.

2. You must pay an amount of income tax and/or capital gains tax at least equal to the tax that the charity reclaims on your donations in the tax year (currently 28p for each £1 you give).

3. If you pay tax at the higher rate you can claim further tax relief in your self-assessment tax return.

4. If you are unsure whether your donations qualify for Gift Aid tax relief, ask the charity or ask your local tax office for leaflet IR113 Gift Aid.

Importance of the audit trail

Basic requirement

2.24 The Revenue guidance on the new Gift Aid procedures is quite clear:

> Charities must keep sufficient records to show that their tax claims are accurate. In other words, they must keep records that enable them to show:
>
> - an audit trail linking each donation to an identifiable donor who has given a valid Gift Aid donation; and
>
> - that all the other conditions for the relief are satisfied. (Provision of benefits for example.)
>
> If a charity does not keep adequate records it may be required to pay back the Inland Revenue tax reclaimed, with interest. It may also be liable to a penalty under the Self Assessment rules.

The requirement for an audit trail existed under the old limited rules but many charities were unaware of it because they made so little use of Gift Aid. The new wider regime makes it even more important for the Inland Revenue to know that charities are properly on top of the paperwork.

Key elements of the trail

2.25 There is no legal list of what constitutes an adequate audit trail and the Inland Revenue has published some general guidance. Much will depend, of course, on the size of the charity and the frequency and type of donations it receives. It is possible to identify the key elements in the trail and look at these in more detail to try to provide a guide to charities on the type of records they are keeping.

The audit trail should encompass the following.

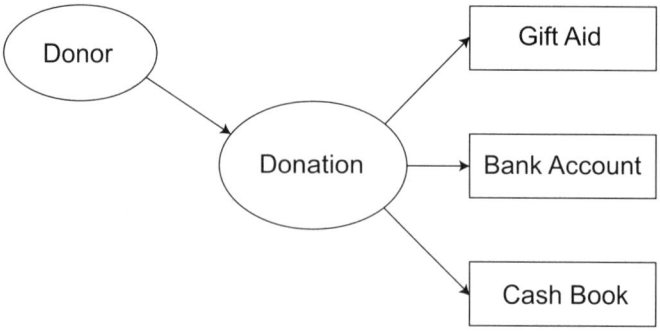

TYING DONOR TO DONATION

2.26 This is the first key stage. There are two important elements:

- identifying the donor;

- clearly linking the donor to the donation.

The donor has to be identified by his or her name and address – this should present no problem as it is basic information that has added to the written declaration and the written record. There is one situation in which care must be taken, and that concerns cheques drawn on a joint bank account where one spouse may be a taxpayer and one not. The Inland Revenue has indicated that, in these circumstances, it will regard the donor as being the person whose name appears on the cheque etc, or who authorises the donation by credit card over the phone, therefore, charities should ensure in such cases that it is always the same person whose name appears on the written declaration and that they are a taxpayer.

The link of donor to donation should be relatively easy where payments are by cheque or debit/credit card or by direct debit, because the name of the donor will appear on documentation of some kind. In the case of card donations or direct debit, that information will be on the charity bank statement or on statements received from credit card companies. In the case of cheques, it might be advisable to take a copy of the cheque or at least to record the details of the cheque in the records.

Cash donations present problems for the charity in any circumstances and clear procedures should be in place aside from the Gift Aid regime in order to ensure completeness in recording cash donations. Linking cash donations to donors will inevitably be the most difficult area of Gift Aid recording and will be the area that will be scrutinised most carefully by the Inland Revenue. It is, therefore, important that charities should consider adopting some suitable recording system and, at the very least, that those who handle cash donations for the charity should be told to ensure that they are meticulous in their recording of the origin of cash donations. Consider various common situations as illustrated below.

Church offerings

2.27 Cash donated on the open plate, or whatever system is used for cash offerings, needs to be identified to donors who might have given open declarations or who might wish to Gift Aid a one-off donation. The only way in which this can be satisfactorily done is through the use of envelopes.

- A donor can simply put their offering in an ordinary envelope on which they have written their name (it would not be unreasonable to assume that the address of regular attenders would be known). The person counting the collection must record on the envelope the amount of cash it contains and record the details in their prime cash record. The envelope should be retained as a prime record itself.

2.28   Gift Aid – the Charity Perspective

- Donors could be provided with pre-printed envelopes which contain a Gift Aid declaration which they complete (see model version above). Again, the amount would need to be recorded and the envelope retained as the written declaration.

- The traditional numbered envelope system can be used. This involves using pre-numbered printed envelopes or ordinary envelopes which bear a designated number. The number is a unique one allocated to a specific donor – in some cases, the number may be allocated by someone other than the treasurer to preserve an element of anonymity. The sum received in the envelope is recorded against that number in the basic records and a record of donations by the individual can be maintained. The Inland Revenue would expect to see a sample of the envelopes used and would also want to inspect the basic recording system to ensure that sums are regularly recorded against numbers.

Sponsored events

2.28 Where cash comes in from sponsored events it is important that the sponsor lists which are provided to participants should have clear details of the individual sponsors and the amounts that they have donated. Those lists should be retained for inspection. It is important that full names and addresses are completed. Often, people seeking sponsorship on their own behalf or on behalf of their children will take sponsor forms to a place of work etc, potential sponsors would, in the past, often simply put their work address and subsequent donors simply use ditto marks. That arrangement will not be valid under the new rules and everyone should be asked to record their home address in full on the form. It might be sensible to record on the form the total cash received which should reconcile to the total of the individual details on the form and also reconcile to the basic cash book records.

Sponsorship money will usually be collected by the participant. Funds may come in the form of cash, cheques made payable to the participant or cheques made payable to the charity. In the first two situations, the participant should bank the money in his or her own account and draw a cheque made payable to the charity and add this to any direct cheques he or she receives. Participants should be encouraged to complete their sponsor forms to show the total amount collected. The charity will want to ensure that this reconciles with the cheque(s) received.

House-to-house collections

2.29 There are two possible ways of satisfying the audit trail requirements.

- The envelopes can be pre-printed with a Gift Aid declaration on which the donor can give details of his or her name and address and either refer to the enclosed amount or a specific amount. In the former case, the person who opens the envelope must record the amount on the envelope and in the records. In the second case, it may be sensible to have some verification on the envelope made at the time the envelope was opened.

- A Gift Aid declaration might be sent with the envelope which could be completed and put into the envelope. Again the opener of the envelopes needs to take action to verify the amount of the donation.

Postal donations

2.30 Charities may receive cash donations through the post. Some may also enclose pre-printed forms included in newspaper adverts, others may have correspondence with them which will enable the donor to be identified. Both types of prime record should be retained.

Street collections

2.31 It is difficult to see how an effective audit trail can be established in these cases without encumbering the collector with so much additional paper. Maybe the advance of technology will eventually allow some system to be introduced. For the present, charities may have to reconcile themselves to the fact that this is an area of income that Gift Aid may not be able to reach.

Cash book

2.32 This is a very important record, particularly in the context of recording cash donations. Treasurers are going to need to be prepared to record more individual donations in the records to tie into the Gift Aid declarations and also the basic evidence of envelopes, sponsor forms etc. If they do not want to record every single pound, but prefer to record a total collection, then they must be prepared to have subsidiary records such as sponsor lists or a list of Gift Aided donations showing names of donor. Either route should be acceptable to the Inland Revenue.

Discipline and routine become the key and any individual who might be involved in the recording system, eg at holiday time, must be aware of what is required.

Bank account

2.33 There are three important areas on which to keep a careful watch:

- bank statements are all-important and should contain essential information such as direct debits received which can identify donors;
- the bank statements will show the total sum banked on any occasion and some record needs to be maintained to ensure that details of all cheques banked are available. These may have been recorded on the paying-in slip but this may not be returned by the bank so make sure that the paying-in stub has been competed in full so that there is a subsidiary record to show the individual cheques that make up the total banking;

- where sums are received from credit card companies, the full breakdown of these sums, showing donors names should be retained.

Gift Aid declarations

2.34 The Gift Aid declaration is the prime record. No repayment claim can be made without it and no matter how much paper is involved, it must be obtained and retained. A number of practical issues arise.

- Charities need to ensure that they have a system in place for obtaining the declarations where donations are received. This can be important where donors respond to appeals and send in donations by post – there should be some automatic response arrangement to secure a declaration wherever possible. Whatever system is used, it needs to be able to cope with large and uneven flows of paper, eg in response to a Christmas appeal or to a famine appeal. Some charities have adopted the procedure of using optical scanning equipment to 'capture' documentation in these circumstances.

- Where a charity holds an open-ended declaration it will need to retain that declaration for as long as it is making reclaims in respect of it. Charities could consider setting up a register of Gift Aid declarations which detail all open declarations and could include information about the donor including:

  (a)   change of name or address details;

  (b)   the date the declaration was made;

  (c)   the date the declaration was cancelled.

- Equally important, it will need to ensure that it is able to 'capture' all donations made by the donor. Some may be easily identified from direct debits or standing order payments. Cheques can be identified and there must be a system for linking cash payments. It may be sensible have a record of donors for each tax year. This basic record, as well as supporting the repayment claim details, may also be useful to the donor. It might be worthwhile sending a record each year of the sums which the charity has included on its repayment claims – this will assist the donors in making their tax return to ensure that they are getting the correct higher-rate relief.

Form of records

2.35 Records do not have to be held on paper. They can be held on computer or stored on microfiche. In the case of computer records, it would be advisable to hold a back-up away from the computer. The Inland Revenue must be able to have access to the records on any inspection visit. The Inland Revenue's view is that the records must be both retrievable and easily accessible by its auditors on any inspection. They will be satisfied in seeing any retrieved images of documents provided they are clear and readable. If there are problems, the charity may be required to produce the originals within a reasonable period of time.

RETENTION OF RECORDS

2.36 The self-assessment rules require that records must be retained for a specified time and these limits are set out below. Charities (other than charities which are companies) may wish to consider retaining records for a longer period. This is because where the Inland Revenue carries out an inspection it may decide to extend the scope of the review to years for which there is no requirement to have retained records. The Inland Revenue likes to use the process of extrapolating the results of a current sample back to earlier years, and this is harder to resist if there is no evidence to support arguments that the figures in earlier years should be lower.

Charities which are trusts

2.37 Charities which are trusts should retain their records until the later of the following dates:

- 31 January next but one after the tax year to which the claim relates. Table 2.3 shows the relevant dates for the next few tax years;

- one year after the date on which the reclaim is made rounded to the next quarter date;

- when the Inland Revenue has completed any audit it has already commenced.

Table 2.3: Retention dates for records

Year of claim	Retention date
2002/03	31 January 2005
2003/04	31 January 2006
2004/05	31 January 2007
2005/06	31 January 2008
2006/07	31 January 2009

Reclaiming tax

Form R68(2000)

2.38 When the new Gift Aid procedures were introduced, the Inland Revenue took the opportunity to simplify the procedures for repayment claims by charities. The old Form R68 was restyled as Form R68(2000) and a new Form R68(New Gift Aid) introduced as a key part of the repayment procedures. Copies of both of these forms are reproduced in the **Appendix** and some practical issues relating to the completion of the forms are set out below.

2.39 Gift Aid – the Charity Perspective

Who makes the claim?

2.39 The claim will usually be made by the charity which receives the donation. There may be circumstances in which a donation is routed through another charity such as a church. The Inland Revenue Guidance Notes cover this and identifies two possible situations.

First, the situation where the church exercises no discretion in collecting the donations and merely acts as a conduit for funds which it passes on to the other charity. In that case, the income never belongs to the church and any claim to Gift Aid must be made by the recipient charity.

The second situation is where the church decides to actively encourage donations and opens up a fund for the purpose. That fund will be a designated fund of the church, and the church will be the donee for Gift Aid purposes and should make the tax reclaim. The Inland Revenue expresses the view that the church should pass on to the end beneficiary charity both the original donation and the tax repayment because this will usually be the expectation of the donor.

When to make a claim

2.40 A claim can be made whenever and as frequently as the charity wants to. The issue really rests on the resources available to complete the forms. Large charities will continue to make frequent claims, but smaller charities will now be able to make claims more frequently; quarterly might be a reasonable option to consider. The option to improve the cash flow position of the charity has been considerably enhanced.

Revenue repayment procedures

2.41 The Inland Revenue approach to making repayments has been simplified in recent years. The attitude is very much 'repay now, check later' – with repayments being made without any delay but with the Inland Revenue reserving the right to carry out an investigation into the background to the claim at a later date. A charity cannot be certain that its claim has been accepted just because repayment has been made, and an investigation that discovered irregularities could result in a substantial bill for back tax, interest and penalties. The Inland Revenue approach to investigations is considered in more detail in **Chapter 9**.

Completion of Form R68(2000)

2.42 The basic repayment form has four sections which require completion.

- **Part 1 – amount of repayment claim**

    This is a summary of the various parts of the claim comprising:

(a) tax reclaimed on other income received under deduction of tax – details of this income should be entered on a separate schedule R68(F);

(b) tax reclaimed in respect of new Gift Aid (see **2.43** below);

(c) the total of the claims on these schedules is then entered.

The charity must also show in this part if it has accepted declarations for payments under the new Gift Aid by telephone.

● **Part 2 – charity details**

This part of the form asks for basic information about the charity, to confirm the name of the charity and whether or not it is a company.

● **Part 3 – repayment details**

This part of the form requires an identification of the repayment period and then concentrates on the mechanics of payment. Possible routes available are:

(a) direct to bank/building society – this is the route that the Inland Revenue wants to encourage and they will make payment direct under the BACS process provided that they have details of the account involved. Space exists on the form to provide that information;

(b) to a nominee – in which case details are required of the nominee;

(c) by cheque to the charity – it will normally be assumed that this should be sent to the address shown on the claim form unless another address is provided by the charity.

● **Part 4 – declaration**

The Inland Revenue requires the form to be completed by an authorised official of the charity. They have been sending out to charities a form on which the authorised official can be detailed and which will show their signature. This official can be changed by the charity, but care needs to be taken that authorisation is always in existence for someone to make a claim. The Inland Revenue will check the signature on the Form R68 with the signature which is held for the authorised official.

The final part of the form requires a signed declaration by the authorised official that, to the best of their knowledge and belief, the information on the form is correct and that the charity is exempt from tax in respect of the income shown on the form. Above the signature box there is an ominous warning which states: 'I understand that false statements can lead to prosecution.'

Completion of Form R68(New Gift Aid)

2.43 The form comprises three columns in which are detailed:

● the name of the donor;

2.43 Gift Aid – the Charity Perspective

- the date of payment or the last payment for which a claim is being made where there has been a series of payments;

- the total of donations received from that donor in the claim period.

In each case, the charity must hold a declaration to cover the donations.

At the bottom of the claim, all the donations are added together and then the tax reclaim is calculated as:

Total donations × 22/78.

Chapter 3   Gift Aid – the Donor's Perspective

Introduction

3.1   The main advantage of Gift Aid for the charity fundraiser is that it not only provides a tax uplift for the charity in securing a 28% tax rebate, it also provides tax incentives for the individual donor. Where the donor is a company, the charity receives a gross payment but the corporate donor can obtain tax relief. Since 2000 the Government has looked at ways to provide greater incentives to donors in a bid to encourage more people to use Gift Aid. Charities need to understand how the system operates from the donor's perspective because that can be used to their advantage to increase the level of giving from particular donors.

This chapter explains the legal background to Gift Aid from the donor angle – first for personal donors and then for corporate donors. It also highlights the areas that charities need to concentrate on in their fundraising programmes to try to extract the maximum advantage from the rules.

The individual donor

The basic legislation

3.2   The basic legislation from the individual donor's point of view is set out in the *Finance Act 1990, s 25(6)* which states:

> Where any gift made by the donor in a year of assessment is a qualifying donation, then, for that year—
>
> (a)   the Income Tax Acts and the Taxation of Chargeable Gains Act 1992 shall have effect, in their application to him, as if
>
>   (i)   the gift had been made after deduction of income tax at the basic rate.

What this means is that the donor is effectively obtaining basic-rate tax relief in respect of each qualifying donation at the time he or she makes that donation. So if an individual makes a donation of £100, the donor is treated for income tax purposes as if he or she has made a gross payment of £128.20 and has deducted basic-rate tax of £128.20 x 22% = £28.20 from that payment. The charity is deemed to have received the gross sum and that is why, as a non-taxpayer, the charity can reclaim the tax of £28.20 that it has suffered.

The donor as a taxpayer

3.3   The Inland Revenue is not in the business of repaying tax that no one has ever paid. If the charity is to claim a repayment then it is important that *someone* should have paid some tax. It is, therefore, one thing for the donor to receive tax relief, but it is also vital that the donor should have a pool of tax out of which that relief can be taken and which will effectively cover the tax which the charity is going to be repaid.

Under the pre-2000 rules, it was essential for the donor to be a basic-rate tax-payer and to have paid sufficient income tax at the basic rate to cover the basic-rate tax 'deducted' in making the gift to the charity under Gift Aid. This was starting to cause problems with the initial introduction of a lower rate of tax of 20% and then in 1999/2000 of a starting rate of 10%.That problem has been resolved in the new regime by taking as the basic requirement that the donor should have paid in total sufficient income tax and capital gains tax to cover the tax treated as deducted from the gift. This is an important change for two reasons.

First, it removes all the complications caused by rates of income tax below the basic rate. All that is necessary is to consider the total tax paid in the year and compare that to the total tax 'deducted' from qualifying donations.

EXAMPLE 3.1

An individual makes a series of qualifying donations to charity during the year 2004/05 which total £1,200. The basic-rate tax deemed to have been deducted in the course of making these payments will be £338.46. The individual must pay total tax of at least that sum which, assuming a basic personal allowance of £4,745 and a full starting rate band of £2,020, the individual must have income of at least £7,386. This will give £2,020 taxable at 10% and £621 at 22% making £338.62 in total.

The calculation must be done for each individual but, for the tax year 2004/05, assuming the individual is entitled to the personal allowance of £4,745, and then the starting rate band of £2,020 taxable at 10%, the minimum levels of income required to avoid any problems of underpaying tax on the qualifying donations are as shown in the table below.

Table 3.1: Minimum income required for donor

| Net payment | Assuming a basic rate of 22% | | Total income of donor |
| | Tax reclaimed | Value to charity | |
£	£	£	£
1	0.28	1.28	4,748
10	2.82	12.82	4,774
50	14.10	64.10	4,886
100	28.20	128.20	5,027
250	70.51	320.51	5,451
500	141.02	641.02	6,156
1,000	282.05	1,282.05	7,130
5,000	1,410.25	6,410.25	12,258

Second, it allows individuals who consistently make capital gains in excess of the annual capital gains tax (CGT) exemption (£8,200 for 2004/05) to make donations to charity out of the proceeds. It would also allow an individual who made a windfall profit out of the sale of an asset to benefit a charity with some of the proceeds.

EXAMPLE 3.2

An individual who owns a property sells it for £100,000 and makes a capital gain of £50,000 after all reliefs and annual exemption. The CGT due on that disposal will be £20,000. If the individual wanted the charity to benefit by the maximum possible amount from the proceeds, he or she could pay up to £70,000 of the proceeds.

£70,000 grossed up at 22% would give a total donation of £89,744, with basic-rate tax of £19,744 being treated as deducted.

Higher-rate relief

3.4 The new regime continues the relief for higher rate taxpayers on the sums paid as qualifying donations. The specific legislation in the *Finance Act 1990, s 25(6)* goes on to state that the Taxes Acts shall have effect as if:

> (ii) the basic rate limit were increased by an amount equal to the grossed up amount of the gift.

This is the effective way of giving higher-rate relief. In calculating their tax liability the donor simply increases the amount of their basic-rate band by the gross amount of gift aid payments made in the tax year.

EXAMPLE 3.3

An individual has total income for 2004/05 of £50,000: the tax liability for the year would be calculated as follows:

	£	Tax £
Total income	50,000.00	
Personal allowance	(4,745.00)	
Starting-rate band	(2,020.00)	202.00
Basic-rate band	(29,380.00)	6,463.60
Liable at higher rate	13,855.00	5,542.00
Total tax liability		12,207.60

If the donor had made Gift Aid payments in the year totalling £2,500, that would be equivalent to gross payments of £3,206, and the tax calculation would now look like this:

3.5 Gift Aid – the Donor's Perspective

	£	Tax £
Total income	50,000.00	
Personal allowance	(4,745.00)	
Starting rate band	(2,020.00)	202.00
Basic rate band	**(32,586.00)**	**7,168.92**
Liable at higher rate	**10,649.00**	**4,259.60**
Total tax liability		**11,603.52**

The tax liability has been reduced by £577.08 as a result of the higher-rate relief for the Gift Aid donations.

The calculation of the higher-rate relief could be done much more quickly by simply taking 18% of the gross amount of the Gift Aid donations. The maximum relief is 40% of the total gross payment, relief of 22% has been obtained by simply making a cash payment of £2,500 and the balance of relief to be given is therefore simply 18% of the gross.

The definition of a higher-rate taxpayer will, of course, vary each year as the tax allowances and the rate bands vary. For 2004/05 the higher-rate threshold is £36,415 being the amount of the basic personal allowance (£4,745) plus the amounts of the starting and basic rate bands (£31,400).

Again, it is possible to set out the level of higher-rate relief in summary tabular form – see Table 3.2.

Table 3.2: Higher-rate relief on qualifying donations

Net payment	Assuming a basic rate of 22%		Higher-rate taxpayer	
	Tax reclaimed	Value to charity	Higher-rate relief	Net cost to donor
£	£	£	£	£
1	0.28	1.28	0.23	0.77
10	2.82	12.82	2.31	7.69
50	14.10	64.10	11.54	38.46
100	28.20	128.20	23.07	76.93
250	70.51	320.51	57.69	192.31
500	141.02	641.02	115.38	384.62
1000	282.05	1,282.05	230.77	769.23
5000	1,410.25	6,410.25	1,153.84	3,846.16

Method of giving relief

3.5   The donor will need to include details of qualifying donations on his or her tax return and will usually receive tax relief through his or her self assessment using the basis of calculation shown in **Example 3.3** above. The relief will be delayed effectively until the filing date for the tax return. For example if a donation is made on 7 May 2004, ie in the tax year 2004/05, the higher-rate relief will not be actually received until the filing date for the 2004/05 return on 31 January 2006. It may be possible to obtain relief earlier if the donor is able to make an election to reduce payments on account.

The Government has partially recognised the problem of delay by introducing a measure which makes it possible to take the higher-rate relief back to the previous year of assessment provided that the donation is made before the tax return for the earlier year has been filed. This has the effect of giving almost instant tax relief in some cases. In the example in the previous paragraph it would be possible to relate the higher-rate tax relief on the 7 May donation back to the previous year 2003/04 where the tax return filing date and final tax payment date is 31 January 2005. The same effect could be obtained for a donation made, say, on 15 January 2005 provided that the tax return for 2003/04 has not already been filed.

Provisional relief could, however, be obtained by employees and directors through the inclusion of the relief in the tax code used to calculate tax deductible under the PAYE system.

Where the donor does not usually receive a tax return, and is not, in consequence in the self-assessment system, the donor should contact his or her tax district to ensure that he or she can make a claim to higher relief that may be due.

Record-keeping

3.6   As a practical point, donors who make more than one donation to charity in a year, either because they benefit a number of charities or because they have made a series of qualifying donations to one charity, should ensure that they have records of the payments made to support any claim made on their tax return. The rules of self assessment require a record to be maintained to support every entry on a tax return and, if there are no records, the Inland Revenue could refuse the claim to higher-rate relief.

Donors need to establish the habit of taking copies of all Gift Aid declarations for single donations, particularly if those donations are made in cash. Where they have previously made declarations which cover a series of donations or are open-ended, donors need to ensure that they record the specific payments which have been made. Bank statements or credit card statements will provide a useful reminder. Again, a reminder to charities who have donors with open-ended declarations might wish to consider giving each such donor a list of the payments which have qualified in the year. This helps the record-keeping and might be a subtle reminder that more could be given.

A boost to giving

3.7   The charity, of course, gets no direct benefit from the higher-rate relief. Its own tax repayment is determined quite independently of the tax status of the donor.

3.8 Gift Aid – the Donor's Perspective

Charities can, however, obtain some benefit by encouraging the higher-rate taxpayer to increase the net amount he or she is prepared to donate whilst actually leaving the individual, after higher-rate tax relief, paying out the same sum as originally.

EXAMPLE 3.4

A 40% taxpayer who, as a basic-rate taxpayer, was paying a net qualifying donation of £1,000 would, as a higher-rate taxpayer, be obtaining higher-rate relief of £230.77 for 2004/05, making the net cost to himself of the payment only £769.23. If the donor was content to retain a net of tax outlay of £1,000, the donor could increase the net sum paid to the charity to £1,300.

The charity would receive a gross sum of £1,667 compared to the £1,282 it received before.

The donor receives higher-rate relief of £300 (£1,667 x 18%) leaving the actual cost to the donor at £1,000.

Observation of a variety of examples of charity fundraising literature suggests that many charities are missing a major opportunity here. Most will say somewhere in their literature that 'higher-rate tax relief may be available on the donation'; very few will actually spell out the basis on which that relief can be obtained or make the basic point that the amount of the actual donation could be increased and the net effect of the higher-rate relief would be to leave the donor paying the sum that they really thought they were parting with. The cash effect for the charity would be an increase of 30% in the cash value of a donation, and that surely makes the effort of some extra wording on a document worthwhile.

Charities: to get the most out of your higher-rate donor base …

- remind them about the higher-rate relief;
- tell them about the carry back of higher-rate relief;
- help them with their record-keeping and at the same time;
- remind them how much they are actually giving and then;
- tell them they could give you 30% more without it costing them anything.

Donor paying insufficient tax

3.8 There is clearly an issue where the donor is not a taxpayer or does not pay sufficient tax to cover the tax deducted on the donation. In these circumstances the position is quite clear. The charity will not suffer in any way if they make a reclaim in respect of the tax. It is entitled to do that and the Inland Revenue will repay the sum without question. The problem is one which falls only on the donor. *Finance Act 1990, s 25(8)* states:

Where the tax treated as deducted from a gift by virtue of *subsection (6)* above exceeds the amount of income tax and capital gains tax with which the donor is charged for the year of assessment, the donor shall be assessable and chargeable with income tax at the basic rate on so much of the gift as is necessary to recover an amount of tax equal to the excess.

In practice, it is likely that this will be achieved through the donor's self-assessment calculation which, in these circumstances, should throw up an underpayment of tax for the year. This is why the charity is required to warn the donor about the need to pay sufficient tax. All charities should reinforce this point with potential donors in their fundraising literature.

There is also a practical need to keep reminding individuals who have given open-ended declarations of the requirement to pay tax. It may be that a declaration given several years before by a donor who was then a taxpayer is no longer viable because they have either ceased to be a taxpayer or are no longer paying sufficient tax to cover their donations.

Residency of donors

3.9 The old Gift Aid rules had a requirement that the donor should be a UK resident individual. This contrasted with the deed of covenant arrangements that allowed a non-resident to be a donor provided he or she paid sufficient UK tax to cover the basic-rate tax on the covenanted payments. The new rules bring the Gift Aid provisions into line (albeit as an afterthought). *Finance Act 1990, s 25(2)(1)* states:

either

  (i) at the time the gift is made, the donor is resident in the United Kingdom or performs duties which by virtue of *s 132(4)(a)* of the *Income and Corporation Taxes Act 1988* (Crown employees serving abroad) are treated as being performed in the United Kingdom; or

  (ii) the grossed up amount of the gift would, if in fact made, be payable out of profits or gains brought into charge to income tax or capital gains tax.

So an individual who is not resident in the UK, but who has income or gains assessable in the UK, would be able to make qualifying donations. This will help UK individuals who go abroad to work, perhaps leaving a property in the UK which is let and generates taxable income. It will also cover a non-resident individual who has some income in the UK through a trade or profession.

Donations by companies

Introduction

3.10 Companies are an increasingly important source of funding for charities and can benefit charities in a number of ways – of which Gift Aid is one.

3.11   Gift Aid – the Donor's Perspective

Companies do not pay income tax – they pay corporation tax – and so the method of dealing with Gift Aid for companies has to be different. Several different approaches have been tried but the approach now in place is basically simple and easy to operate. The type of payment is common to all companies but there is a difference in the way relief is given depending on whether or not the company is controlled by a charity.

Gross payments

3.11   Company Gift Aid payments are made gross. If a company wishes to make a payment of £1,000 to charity it will pay that sum over directly. The charity receives the gross sum and will not have to go through the procedure of making a tax reclaim. Simplicity is the order of the day and charities should be encouraging companies to make Gift Aid donations.

The paperwork is also very simple. No declaration is required. The charity simply needs to record the donation in its accounting records and the company needs to record the payment and if, possible, retain some evidence, such as a charity receipt, to show that the payment was made for charitable purposes.

How the company gets relief

3.12   The charity clearly benefits by receiving a gross payment – how does the company get any relief? The qualifying donation is not allowable in arriving at the taxable profits from the company trade or investments. The relief is given normally in the company accounting period in which the payment is actually made except in certain cases where the company is controlled by a charity (**3.13**). It is given as a charge against the total profits assessable to corporation tax and is regarded as what is known as a 'non-trade charge'. The significance of this definition is that if the company makes a loss or has profits less than the qualifying donations made, it will not be able to carry forward those unrelieved donations to a following year and so, effectively, will receive no tax relief on the payments.

EXAMPLE 3.5

Megabucks Ltd makes a donation to charity of £100,000 in July 2003. This falls in its financial year to 31 March 2004. Its total profits from its trading activities in that year are £1million. Its corporation tax computation will show:

Trading profits	£1,000,000
Less donations	£100,000
Net taxable	£900,000

If its trading position deteriorated after it had made the donation, the situation might be that its profits for the year were a mere £50,000. The computation will then be:

Trading profits	50,000
Less donations	50,000
Net taxable	nil

The balance of qualifying donations of £50,000 will be lost and no relief will be possible.

If the company actually made a loss, then there would be no relief for the qualifying donations.

Companies controlled by charities – a carry back relief

3.13   There are situations where, in order to get around a restriction for tax exemption for certain trading activities, a charity may decide to run the trade through a separate company which it controls. The simple approach is for the company to make a payment to the charity equal to its profits so that the charity effectively receives the benefits of the income from the trading activity without running the risk that the Inland Revenue will not grant tax exemption to that income. (In practice, there may be problems with this approach and charities should take advice in this area.) If the basic rules described at **3.11** above were to apply, this could lead to some difficulties because it may not be possible to ascertain the amount of the company profit and hence the Gift Aid payment before the end of the accounting period. There would then be a mismatch between profits and payments that could lead to some payments being charged to corporation tax and some Gift Aid payments not being given tax relief.

To get around this problem, the legislation now states that where a company is wholly owned by a charity, and that company makes a qualifying donation to a charity, it can claim for the whole or part of the payment it makes to be treated as a charge on income in an accounting period falling wholly or partly within a period of nine months ending with the date of the donation. Put another way, the company has nine months from the end of its accounting period to make the payment and have it treated as a charge of that accounting period. These provisions are by virtue of *ICTA 1988, s 339(7AA)*.

EXAMPLE 3.6

A company wholly owned by a charity has an accounting period ending on 31 December 2004. It wants to make a payment to the charity and by the time it has accurately calculated its taxable profits for that accounting period, it is 10 April 2005 before it is able to make the payment. It will be able to relate that payment, made out of the profits of the year to 31 December 2004, to that accounting period. If it failed to make the payment by 1 October 2005 it would not be able to make the carry back.

3.14   Gift Aid – the Donor's Perspective

Company owned by a charity – definition

3.14 The definition set out in *ICTA 1988, s 339(7AB)* requires that if the company is a company with ordinary share capital, every share must be owned by a charity or charities. If it is a company limited by guarantee, then every person who can beneficially participate in the divisible profits of the company, or is beneficially entitled to assets in the event of a winding up, must be a charity or a company wholly owned by a charity.

Chapter 4   Gift Aid – the Problem of Donor Benefit

Introduction

An awareness of the problem

4.1   On the face of it, the Gift Aid legislation is very wide and encourages giving in a variety of situations. It is not, however, a *carte blanche* which can allow anything paid to a charity to be treated as a donation. The legislation had safeguards written into the first version back in 1990 and those safeguards were strengthened in the 2000 version. It must be said that there was very little awareness of the benefits rules among the charity community prior to 2000. That awareness has increased, but the level of ignorance remains at a worryingly high level and charities only seem to become aware of the problem when the Inland Revenue points it out to them. The Inland Revenue has published some very clear guidance on the issue in particular on the charity pages of its website and charities cannot simply claim ignorance of the issues.

Basic impact of the legislation

4.2   The benefit rules have a statutory basis in the *Finance Act 1990, s 25(2)(e)*. This includes as a condition of a payment satisfying the requirements to be treated as a Gift Aid payment that:

> … neither the donor nor any person connected with them receives a benefit in consequence of making it or, where the donor or person connected with him does receive a benefit in consequence of making it the relevant value of the gift does not exceed the limit imposed by *subsection (5A)* below and the amount to be taken into account for the purposes of this paragraph in relation to the gift does not exceed £250.

If this condition is infringed, then the whole of the payment made falls to be excluded from the Gift Aid regime. Charities must, therefore, be aware of three important issues.

● What constitutes a benefit?

● Who are individuals who may be 'connected' to the donor?

● What are the values of benefits which will cause a problem?

The answers to these questions must always be considered in the specific context of the charity and its activities.

What is a benefit?

What form can a benefit take?

4.3   Benefits can arise in many different ways. At one level a charity may simply wish to give a donor some token of appreciation or acknowledgement for the their donation – that should generally cause few problems. At the other extreme, a charity provides a positive incentive to a donor to make a donation, eg 'if you give us a donation above a certain figure we will give you something which is relatively small in relation to the donation but is nevertheless worth having'. In between comes the complex area of benefits that may result from the membership of a charity.

A benefit could take the form of goods provided. It could be in the form of services rendered. In some instances it could be something even more intangible. For example, in the past the Inland Revenue indicated that if an individual donor was released from a deed of covenant to allow him or her to make Gift Aid payments, that could be a benefit because the individual had been released from a legal obligation. The Inland Revenue has indicated that it will not be pursuing this line in the context of the new regime, but the example serves to illustrate the point.

In consequence of making the gift

4.4   This is an important phrase in the legislation because it indicates that there must be a clear link between the making of the gift and the provision of the benefit. The benefit must be received as a consequence of making the gift. There must be some link between the making of the gift and the provision of the benefit, but the benefit does not have to be provided directly by the charity – it could come from a third party.

The phrase also indicates that the order of the events must be (i) gift then (ii) benefit. This can be important where someone decides to make a donation to charity as a token of appreciation for some service received by himself or herself or a relative. For example, the family of a patient who has been cared for in a hospice may decide to make a donation to that hospice after the death of their relative. There will be no problem in this case because the benefit which the relative received cannot be argued to be in consequence of the donation. If, however, they were to have made the donation during their relative's lifetime, there would be an argument that the benefit of care was received as a consequence of the donation.

One further point to be noted is that there is no time limit between the donation and the benefit. The author has seen a case where an arts charity about to embark on a major renovation of its facilities offered donors a number of benefits depending on the level of their donations. For example, a donation of £500 would secure receipt of free tickets for performances a year and two years ahead. The Inland Revenue confirmed in a discussion on this 'hypothetical case' that they would seek to invoke the benefit rules (assuming that the values were relevant). The time period was irrelevant – the benefit 'was in consequence' of the donation. The Inland Revenue also indicated that if the charity had made no mention of the free tickets in the publicity for the donations, but had then decided that they would give all donors who gave above a certain level tickets for events, there would not have been a problem.

Examples of benefits which may be caught

4.5   The range of potential benefits which might be given by a charity is enormous, and numerous examples have been seen. The summaries at **4.6–4.10** below give a flavour of what might happen – all have to be seen as subject to the 'relevant value' rules which are described at **4.26** below. They all point to the care that charities must take, particularly in fundraising literature in describing what benefits might result to the donor. At **4.29** below, a number of very specific problems will be discussed once all the rules relating to benefits have been considered.

FREE OR DISCOUNTED SERVICES OR FACILITIES PROVIDED BY THE CHARITY

4.6   In return for the donation the charity will offer free tickets to future events put on by the charity or admission at a substantial discount. If the publicity clearly links the free tickets to the donation – particularly if the number of free tickets is linked directly to the size of the donation – then there is a clear benefit. See **4.11** below which discusses the circumstances in which free admission will not be regarded as a benefit.

DONATIONS LINKED TO FUNDRAISING EVENTS

4.7   The charity runs a fundraising event such as a gala dinner or a charity film prèmiere and offers donors a meal or tickets and a meal in return for a donation which is well in excess of what the meal/tickets would actually cost. In these circumstances, there is a clear benefit being provided in consequence of the donation. See **4.31** below for a way in which the benefit problem can be minimised in such cases.

If a donation is linked to some kind of acknowledgement, eg in an event programme or on a plaque, the Inland Revenue accepts that there is no benefit in this type of situation. The wording in such a case should be limited to thanking the donor for support and adding the donor's name and/or the corporate logo. Straying beyond these limits could be regarded by the Inland Revenue as offering advertising or promotion in some way and a benefit could arise.

BENEFITS OF MEMBERSHIP

4.8   This is a potential minefield. Where the member pays his or her subscription and seeks to apply the Gift Aid rules, then the charity must look closely at what the member actually receives in return for his or her subscription. The Inland Revenue would accept that the right to vote in an AGM would not be a benefit. The receipt of literature such as the annual report and accounts, regular newsletters, programmes of events, etc would strictly be a benefit, but would be one which the Inland Revenue would accept as having a nil value. Where membership includes the right to receive free a magazine, which would also be available to the public but at a price, then there is a benefit which has a measurable value. The Inland Revenue will accept that membership which does not secure a right to personal use of facilities provided by the charity – as distinct from a general right of members – would not cause a problem.

The right of free admission is a clear benefit and must be valued except in the cases which are described at **4.11** below.

Membership often includes the right to obtain other services and facilities at a discount. This could include discounted car insurance, special deals on loan interest, reduced costs of books. All of these are clearly benefits. The issue then becomes one of valuation which is discussed at **4.22** below.

SUPPORT FOR CHARITY WORKERS

4.9 This is a very difficult area. The scenario might be that the donor provides support to a missionary society or an aid agency to directly provide for the needs of a specific individual who is a worker with that charity. If that worker is not related in any way to the donor there is no problem. If, however, the worker is related in one of the ways which connects the worker to the donor, then there is a potential benefit issue to be considered. The worker is benefiting directly in consequence of the donation. This will be discussed in more detail at **4.20** below.

SAVING TAX

4.10 This may seem an unusual benefit but the point was taken by the Inland Revenue in a case before the Special Commissioners in 1997. The case was *St Dunstan's v Major [1997] STC (SCD) 212*. A Mr Webber, who was the sole beneficiary under the will of his mother, entered into a deed of variation under which a donation of £20,000 was made to a charity, St Dunstan's. A deed of variation allows the will of a deceased person to be varied within two years of the date of death, and must be agreed in writing by all those beneficiaries under the will who will be affected by the variation. It is regarded as having been effected by the deceased for inheritance tax (IHT) purposes and the calculation of IHT on the death has to be reworked.

In this case, the only beneficiary affected was Mr Webber, and he was able to effect the deed very easily. Because the revised will provided for a donation to charity, which is exempt for IHT, the total liability due on the estate was reduced by £8,000 (£20,000 × 40%). Once the administration of the estate was complete, the sum of £20,000 was paid to the charity. Mr Webber then signed a Gift Aid certificate, and the charity made a repayment claim of £6,667 in respect of the tax due on the Gift Aid payment. It was this claim that was contested before the Special Commissioner.

The Inland Revenue put forward two grounds for refusing the claim. The first, that the gift had not been made by an individual, was rejected by the Special Commissioner. He pointed out that although the deed of variation was deemed to have been made by the deceased for IHT purposes, that was not the case for other purposes. Mr Webber had bound himself to make the payment to the charity and had done so when the estate had been wound up.

The second argument from the Inland Revenue was that, as a result of making the gift, a benefit had been received by Mr Webber. It was pointed out that the legislation does not state that the benefit has to be provided by the charity – the wording refers to a benefit received by the donor.

The Commissioner concluded that since Mr Webber was the sole beneficiary of the estate, any reduction in IHT liability must ultimately have benefited him. The benefit arose directly as a result of the Gift Aid payment and that payment could not qualify for relief.

On the face of it, this may seem a harsh decision because Mr Webber had received £20,000 less by way of inheritance as a result of the deed. Without the deed, he would have received net of IHT the sum of £202,000. As a result of the deed, he actually received £190,202. Looked at another way, however, if Mr Webber had received the net estate of £202,000 and had then paid out the gift of £20,000, his net receipt would only have been £182,200. He had benefited by £8,000.

Exemption for right of admission in certain cases

BASIC PROVISION

4.11 One common benefit of membership of a charitable organisation is the right of free admission to property owned by the charity or to exhibitions mounted by the charity. The legislation relating to deeds of covenant provided some exemptions in this area to allow membership to be covenanted and those relaxed provisions are being introduced for Gift Aid purposes. *Finance Act 1990, s 25(5E)* reads:

> In determining whether a gift to a charity falling within *subsection (5F)* below is a qualifying donation there shall be disregarded the benefit of any right of admission received in consequence of making the gift—
>
> (a) to view property the preservation of which is the sole or main purpose of the charity; or
>
> (b) to observe wildlife the conservation of which is the sole or main purpose of the charity;
>
> but this subsection shall not apply unless the opportunity to make gifts which attract such a right is available to members of the public.

4.12   Gift Aid – the Problem of Donor Benefit

It should be pointed out that the relaxation applies only to admission to view – it would not cover admission to a music event at the property, or to a discount for purchases.

WHICH CHARITIES QUALIFY?

4.12 *Finance Act 1990, s 25(5F)* reinforces the point that charities which may benefit from this rule must have the sole or main object of preservation of property or conservation of wildlife for the public benefit. The Inland Revenue accepts that for these purposes 'property' covers more than real estate. The preservation of artefacts and paintings is regarded as the preservation of property. Conservation of wildlife would include plants and trees as well as animals and birds.

The important wording in the charity's objects must be a reference to preservation and conservation. The Inland Revenue guidance gives examples of three situations which would not qualify for the favourable treatment.

- A church whose sole or main purpose is the advancement of religion (and not the preservation of buildings) may hold its services in an historic church building. When services are not being held, the church may charge people to view the property. The Inland Revenue's view is that the church is not a heritage charity and the relaxation does not apply.

- A charitable school (its main purpose advancement of education) may carry out that education in an historic building. During non-term time it may charge people to view the building, but the relaxation will not apply because the objects are not heritage or conservation.

- A university may have an art gallery with significant paintings in it or a botanical garden with specimen plants, but since its objects are advancement of education and not heritage/conservation, the relaxation cannot apply.

The Inland Revenue points out that, in each of these cases, it might be possible to consider the establishment of a separate charity with specific heritage/conservation/preservation objects to hold the property. Whether the institution would want to go to those lengths, with all the extra administration involved, may be debatable.

WHICH PAYMENTS QUALIFY

4.13 The Inland Revenue makes it quite clear that a payment for admission is not a donation and cannot qualify. However, the payment of a donation which then allows free admission would qualify. Similarly, membership which does not breach the rules outlined in **4.8** above would also qualify.

The practical impact of this clause is to allow benefits which may actually exceed the value of the donation to fall outside the benefit rules. Typically, a family only need to visit four National Trust properties during a year to get full value (as measured in normal admission prices) from their annual subscription.

The right of admission is further qualified by the *Finance Act 1990, s 25(5G)* which refers to the right as meaning:

> … admission of the person making the gift (or any member of his family who may be admitted because of the gift) either free of the charges normally payable for admission by members of the public, or on payment of a reduced charge.

The Inland Revenue Guidance Notes indicate that it regards 'members of the family' as meaning the donor's parents, spouse, children and their spouses. The guidance also accepts that charities may limit free admission to a maximum number of people in a group and cannot be expected to check the identity of every person entering their premises. It will accept such restrictions on 'family groups' as satisfying the 'members of the family' test.

A CURRENT PROBLEM

4.14   The opportunities afforded by the 'admission' relaxation were quickly seized upon after 2000 as a way of improving the finances of many charities. Charities decided to encourage donations or effectively offered a day membership and then gave free admission. There was administrative work involved because the donation had to be made before any admission process took place and the audit trail for Gift Aid purposes had to be established, which meant that the donor had to complete a declaration. For some charities, the sheer paperwork or the scale of admissions rendered the benefits a step too far, but many charities have taken advantage of the arrangements. For the donor it might mean obtaining higher-rate tax relief by taking the family to the zoo for the day!

In fact, it seems that too many charities have been taking advantage and, at the time of writing (Summer 2004), there is a process of consultation going on to consider changes to the rules and subsequent legislation may follow.

Which individuals are caught?

The donor

4.15   This is clear and straightforward – if the person making the donation receives a benefit in excess of the limits, then the gift is negated for Gift Aid purposes.

Persons connected with the donor

INDIVIDUALS

4.16   The issue of connection was considered briefly in **Chapter 2** in the context of purchases, and the same rules apply here. First of all, it is necessary to identify those individuals deemed to be 'connected' with the donor for these purposes. The legislation uses the definition of 'connected person' in *ICTA 1988, s 839*.

This is a wide definition setting out that 'a person' is connected with all the following persons.

An individual who is their wife or husband, or is a relative, or the wife or husband of a relative of the individual or of the individual's wife or husband. Relative means brother, sister, ancestor or lineal descendant.

Shown in diagrammatic form the connections which are significant become more apparent.

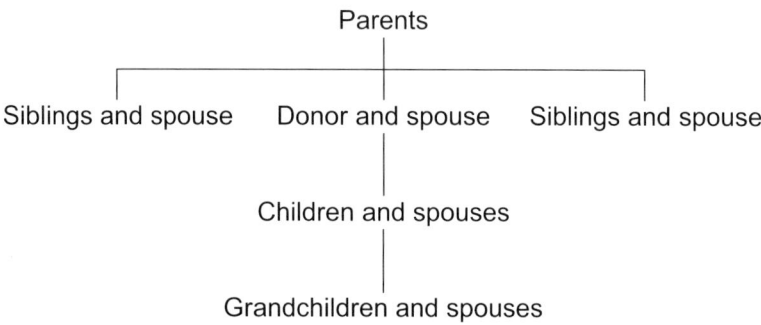

There are some family connections which are not caught – for example, uncle and nephew.

COMPANY

4.17 The rules on benefits apply where a benefit is received either by the company or a 'connected person'. This latter phrase is helpfully further clarified by the *Finance Act 1990, s 25(7A)* which identifies a connected person as:

... a person connected with—

(a) the company; or

(b) a person connected with the company.

The legislation refers to definitions in *ICTA 1988, s 839*, which states:

(6) A company is connected with another person if that person has control of it, or if that person and persons connected with him together have control of it.

(7) Any two or more persons acting together to secure or exercise control of a company shall be treated in relation to that company as connected with one another and with any person acting on the directions of any of them to secure or exercise control of the company.

The definition of 'control' is found in *ICTA 1988, s 416* and, in simple terms, means that the person owns the greater part of the ordinary share capital of the company, although the definition does actually go further than this.

In practical terms it is therefore necessary to identify who is connected to the company. In the case of public companies, this will not usually be a relevant issue unless there is exceptionally a 51% shareholder or a connected 51% shareholding group. The situation will always be relevant in considering donations made by family controlled companies or so called 'owner managed companies'.

EXAMPLE 4.1

Goodacre Ltd makes a donation to a charity of £500 as a result of which Frank Goodacre who owns 75% of the shares becomes entitled to attend a gala premiere of the latest Julia Roberts movie. Frank is clearly a person connected to the company and the benefit rules must be considered. They must also be considered if the person attending the dinner was not Frank, but his son Albert.

So if as a result of the donation, any connected person receives a benefit in excess of the legal limits the effect would be to nullify the Gift Aid effects of the donation. How might such benefits arise?

SCHOOL FEE PAYMENTS

4.18 Direct payment of school fees via Gift Aid is an obvious benefit and will not work. There are a number of schools which have been established outside the traditional private school network where a trust has been established to provide the school, but parents are encouraged to make donations towards specific items. The Inland Revenue publishes some guidance in this area at section 3.45 of their guidance on Gift Aid. They comment as follows:

> Invariably the (Educational) Trust is established to provide education for children as an alternative to State education. Whilst parents may pay for text books, exercise books, exam fees and consumable materials, they are not required to pay any fees to cover the costs of tuition or other overheads.

> The Inland Revenue view of payments made by parents and persons connected to them, to such trusts under the Gift Aid scheme is that the benefit the donor or someone connected to them receives will generally be in excess of the benefit rules.

> The Inland Revenue view is based on the fact that there is a cost in providing education for the child and this cost is met in consequence of the Gift Aid payments being made. This includes the costs of tuition, heating and lighting the premises and other administrative costs which would be taken into account by a private school in setting fees.

> In situations where the trust has a genuine fee structure in place, ie fees are charged in respect of all students and the fees are set at such a level that enables the trust to operate without needing additional support, the Inland Revenue would accept that the benefit of education arises from the payment of the fees. Consequently, the receipt of education would not be received as a consequence of making donations over and above the fees and so those donations could qualify for Gift Aid.

Where there is no fee structure or only nominal fees are charged, insufficient to enable the trust to operate without additional donations we do not accept that the additional donations give rise to no benefit. In considering whether the level of fees was sufficient to cover operating costs we accept that trusts should be allowed to take account of reliable, ongoing sources such as endowments, but not one-off or periodic donations where no binding commitment exists.

Where a parent makes a donation to the school to help fund a capital project such as a new library, there is a potential benefit, but the Inland Revenue will accept that the benefit to the child is likely to be minimal in such a case because the benefit is shared, not just by all current pupils but future pupils as well.

EDUCATIONAL SCHOOL TRIPS

4.19   The Inland Revenue has produced guidance to cover situations where Gift Aid might be used in respect of voluntary contributions towards school educational trips. The Inland Revenue has passed a Guidance Note to the Department of Education, which is included in the advice the department issues to schools. That text is as follows:

In schools, other than independent schools, the education provided wholly or mainly during school hours is free. This means that head teachers may not impose a charge on parents for any visit that is undertaken as part of the National Curriculum and occurs during school hours. The head teacher may, however, ask for a voluntary contribution.

Parents must be made aware that the contribution is not compulsory, and the children of parents who do not contribute may not be discriminated against. It is permissible for the school to ask parents to contribute more than the minimum amount in order to subsidise those pupils whose parents have not contributed. However, if there are not enough voluntary contributions and the shortfall cannot be made up, the visit may have to be cancelled.

Gift Aid

Voluntary parental contributions to charitable schools or charities associated with LEA schools to assist schools to send pupils on educational school trips in school time may be eligible for tax relief under the Gift Aid scheme, provided the usual requirements of the scheme are satisfied and in particular:

● parental contributions are made on the basis that they are **not** refundable (and are not in any event refunded) if the trip does not go ahead or if their child does not go on the trip;

● any benefit arising from the school trip does not exceed the maximum level of permissible benefit for the donation.

For a donation of £0–£100 the value of the benefits must not exceed 25% of the donation. For a donation of £101–£1,000 the value of the benefits must not exceed £25.

Benefits include travel costs, trip insurance, cost of entry and associated educational material, cost of food and drink supplied and any other costs associated with the trip (costs averaged per pupil if appropriate).

In general, however, it is likely that the benefits associated with a school trip contribution will exceed the maximum level of permissible benefits and so the donation will not come within the Gift Aid scheme.

Example 1

The cost of an educational trip to a local museum amounts to £8 (transport £5 entry £2 and brochure £1). The school asks for a voluntary contribution of £10. The payment of £10 cannot be made under the Gift Aid scheme as the benefit of £8 exceeds the 25% limit (80%).

However, provided the requested contribution is not less than the benefits, any payment in excess of the requested contribution can be Gift Aided.

Example 2

The position is the same as in Example 1 but a parent makes a voluntary contribution of £15 instead of the requested £10. The additional £5 can be made as a Gift Aid payment.

MISSIONARY SUPPORT

4.20 It is quite common practice among missionary societies for individual missionaries to have to obtain financial support or to receive such support as a supplement to their remuneration. In some cases this will replace remuneration. It is natural that some of this support will come from family members and if money is given under Gift Aid to the missionary organisation directly to support a relative it will fall foul of the Gift Aid benefit rules. Ironically, it was one of the areas that did get through under a deed of covenant. It is thought that the problem can be overcome by making a general donation to the organisation leaving them to use the money as it sees fit. Alternatively, a donation could be made to a local church which could then decide through its usual decision-making channel to send money to support a particular individual. What is clear is that this is an area which requires considerable care.

SPONSORED ADVENTURE HOLIDAYS

4.21 These have become a feature of charitable fundraising in recent years. A number of charities organise these events which offer the chance to do something very different, eg ride a bike though Nepal whilst raising money for the charity. The usual arrangement is for the participant to pay a non-refundable deposit or registration fee and to then raise a minimum amount of sponsorship in return for going on the trip. The charity pays a third party to arrange the event and this will cover all of the participants' expenses. The question then is whether the sponsorship payments can qualify for Gift Aid.

It is not possible for the participants to use Gift Aid to make any of their payments. They are paying a fee not making a donation. Even if it were to be dressed up as a donation, the benefit rules would disqualify it.

Sponsorship payments from connected parties will also fall foul of the benefit rules and Gift Aid cannot be used for those donations. Payments from friends and colleagues would not be caught and Gift Aid can be used in those situations.

What values of benefits will cause a problem?

How is the benefit valued?

4.22 The test required by the legislation is not that there should be no benefit, but that the value of the benefits which are received in consequence of the gift do not exceed the specific limits. Before considering what those limits are, it is important to consider how a benefit is actually valued – in some cases this may be relatively easy, in others it will not. The Inland Revenue guidance is not particularly helpful. It identifies the issue of goods or services provided to the public by the charity or someone else and makes the obvious point that an arm's length market value can be used. For example, a theatre ticket given in return for a donation will have a clear market price, as does a meal provided at a gala dinner.

PUBLICATIONS

4.23 Where a charity provides a free magazine to members, that magazine may also be available to the public at a specific cover price and that will enable an accurate measure of benefit. Where the magazine is not available and it is produced for the purpose of describing the work of the charity, eg a newsletter, handbook, annual report or programme of events, then the Inland Revenue accepts that it has no value for benefit purposes.

DISCOUNTS

4.24 The benefit received may be that of a discount on normal admissions to a museum or a theatre over the period of the subscription, say, one year. The value of the discount can be accurately calculated because there is an established market price for admission, but is it necessary to consider the theoretical benefit of a discount for every possible performance or exhibition or is it permissible to use hindsight and identify how many times the member took advantage of the discount? The Inland Revenue's view is that the charity should try to ascertain the average take-up of the discount by its membership. This may be possible where the charity has the direct information, eg a discount for purchases made in a museum shop by members of the museum society. It may be harder to do this where the discount is given by a third party, although that party would, presumably, be prepared to give the charity the relevant information.

CHARITY AUCTIONS

4.25 The Inland Revenue give some guidance in this area. It recognises that when an item is purchased at a charity auction, the purchaser may intentionally pay more than the item is worth in order to support the charity. The Inland Revenue would accept, therefore, that the normal market value of the lot can be taken as its value if that is lower than the sale price. That normal value can be compared to the sum received and provided the financial limits are not breached, the sale price may be Gift Aided.

For example, if someone paid £10,000 for a weekend break that was shown in the travel agents brochure as having a cost of £240, there would be no problem.

There can be a problem where the item being auctioned has connections to a celebrity, and the price paid is likely to reflect that. For example, if a pair of shoes worn by a pop star was auctioned and made £10,000, that would represent the market value of those shoes irrespective of the fact that if purchased in a shoe shop they might cost only £150.

Similar issues arise if the item being auctioned has no market value simply because it is a unique event. For example, the right to be a TV producer for a day, or a trip on a Royal Navy frigate. In such situations the Inland Revenue would treat the price paid as being the market value and no Gift Aid would be possible. The same situation would apply for an auction of promises where people offer to carry out specific tasks, eg wash a car for the successful bidder.

Basic relevant value test

4.26 The basic value limits are imposed by a new *subsection (5A)* inserted into the *Finance Act 1990, s 25.* These limits are banded as follows.

Table 4.1: Benefit bands

Amount of donation	Value of benefits
Up to £100	25% of the value of the gift
£101 to £1,000	£25
Over £1,000	2.5% of the gift

These limits apply to each donation and, if they are exceeded, then that donation fails to qualify as a Gift Aid donation. So in simple terms, if a charity decided to hold a gala dinner and charged each person £50, the sums paid would not qualify for Gift Aid unless the actual value of the dinner which each person received was less than £12.50. That might be acceptable if the dinner concerned was a simple bread and cheese meal, but would probably not qualify if the dinner was at a four-star hotel.

4.27 Gift Aid – the Problem of Donor Benefit

The rules go further, however, and require a charity to annualise the value of benefits in certain cases. There is also an overriding limit of £250 which applies to aggregate donations from the same donor in the same tax year. Those provisions will be considered in more detail.

Impact of annualisation

WHEN ANNUALISATION IS NECESSARY

4.27 The concept of annualisation is set out in the *Finance Act 1990, s 25 (5B)–(5D). Subsection (5B)* states that:

> … where a benefit received in consequence of making a gift—
>
> (a) consists of the right to receive benefits at intervals over a period of less than twelve months;
>
> (b) relates to a period of less than twelve months; or
>
> (c) is one of a series of benefits received at intervals in consequence of making a series of gifts at intervals of less than twelve months,

the value of the benefits shall be adjusted for the purposes of *subsection (4)* above and the amount of the gift shall be adjusted for the purposes of *subsection (5A)* above.

In these circumstances both the value of the benefit and the value of the gift are annualised for the purposes of applying the *subsection (5A)* limits.

Subsection (5C) deals with another possible variation:

> Where a benefit, other than a benefit which is one of a series of benefits received at intervals, is received in consequence of making a gift which is one of a series of gifts made at intervals of less than twelve months, the amount of the gift shall be adjusted for the purposes of *subsection (5A)* above.

In this case it is the value of the gift which must be annualised but not the value of the benefit.

It is possible to summarise the four situations where annualisation is necessary as follows:

Table 4.2: Categories of annualisation

Category	Gift	Benefit
1	Single	Several received over interval of less than 12 months
2	Single	Single but related to period of less than 12 months
3	Series over less than 12 months	Series at intervals
4	Series over less than 12 months	Single benefit

HOW ANNUALISATION IS EFFECTED

4.28 This is set out in the legislation in *Finance Act 1990, s 25(5D)* which states that:

> Where the value of a benefit, or the amount of a gift, falls to be adjusted under *subsection (5B)* or *(5C)* above, the value or amount shall be multiplied by 365 and the result shall be divided by—
>
> (a) in the case falling within *subsection (5B)(a)* or *(b)* above, the number of days falling in the period of less than twelve months;
>
> (b) in the case falling within *subsection (5B)(c)* or *(5C)* above, the average number of days in the intervals of less than twelve months.

The Inland Revenue has indicated that where the period or intervals are, in practice, measured in calendar months, then annualisation can be done by reference to calendar months not days.

The Inland Revenue has produced a series of examples in their Guidance Notes showing how annualisation works and it makes sense to consider those examples in detail.

EXAMPLE 4.2

Ms Smith makes four unconnected donations to a charity as follows.

Date	Amount	Benefit
6 May 2003	£30	Nil
21 June 2003	£10	Nil
18 August 2003	£25	Nil
5 February 2004	£80	Book worth £30

There are no benefits associated with the first three gifts and so they will all qualify. The issue concerns the book received in consequence of the fourth gift. The four categories will now be considered.

Category	Gift	Benefit	Example
1	Single	Several received over interval of less than 12 months	Not applicable – single benefit
2	Single	Single but related to period of less than 12 months	Not applicable – not related to a period
3	Series over less than 12 months	Series at intervals	Not applicable – single gift and single benefit
4	Series over less than 12 months	Single benefit	Not applicable – single gift

Annualisation is not required. The value of the benefit needs to be compared only to the amount of the gift. The maximum value permitted for a gift of £80 is 25% or £20, the value of the gift is £30 and exceeds the limit so the gift does not qualify.

EXAMPLE 4.3

Mr Patel makes a single payment of £240 to a charity in consequence of which he receives the right to receive 12 free monthly magazines each worth £2.50. The value of the benefit is therefore £30 (12 × £2.50). Consider the categories:

Category	Gift	Benefit	Example
1	Single	Several received over interval of less than 12 months	Not applicable – interval is 12 months
2	Single	Single but related to period of less than 12 months	Not applicable – interval is 12 months
3	Series over less than 12 months	Series at intervals	Not applicable – single gift
4	Series over less than 12 months	Single benefit	Not applicable – single gift

Again, annualisation does not apply. The relevant value for a gift of £240 is £25 and as the value of the benefit is £30 the gift cannot qualify.

EXAMPLE 4.4

Mrs O'Connor makes a single payment of £120 to a charity, in consequence of which she receives the right to receive six free monthly magazines worth £2.50 each. The right to receive the magazines has a value of £15 (6 × £2.50). Consider the categories:

Category	Gift	Benefit	Example
1	Single	Several received over interval of less than 12 months	Applicable
2	Single	Single but related to period of less than 12 months	Not applicable – series of benefits
3	Series over less than 12 months	Series at intervals	Not applicable – single gift
4	Series over less than 12 months	Single benefit	Not applicable – single gift

Since the condition of Category 1 has been satisfied it is necessary to annualise both the gift and the benefits. The period of the benefit is six months and so both gift and benefit are annualised by the fraction ¹²⁄ – more simply they are each doubled to give an annualised gift of £240 and an annualised benefit of £30. As with Mr Patel in **Example 4.3** above, the relevant value for a gift of £240 should not exceed £25 and the gift therefore fails. Without annualisation, the actual benefit received of £15 would have been within the limit, so if the benefit had been expressed as the right to receive six magazines over a 12-month period there would have been no annualisation and the gift would have qualified. Charities who offer publications as part of a subscription would do well to note the impact and make the offer of benefits accordingly.

EXAMPLE 4.5

Mr Green makes a single payment of £120 to a performing arts charity, in consequence of which he receives the right to a 5% discount on theatre tickets purchased in the next six months. The benefit of the right is worth, say, £15. (The Inland Revenue does not indicate how they might have arrived at that figure in practice – what if Mr Green did not buy any tickets?) Apply the categories as before:

Category	Gift	Benefit	Example
1	Single	Several received over interval of less than 12 months	Not applicable – single benefit
2	Single	Single but related to period of less than 12 months	Applicable – single benefit relating to a six month period
3	Series over less than 12 months	Series at intervals	Not applicable – single gift
4	Series over less than 12 months	Single benefit	Not applicable – single gift

It is interesting that the Inland Revenue views the right to receive the discount as a single benefit rather than a series of benefits – the distinction is academic because annualisation would apply in either case. The period concerned is again six months so the impact of annualisation is to double both gift and benefit to £240 and £30 respectively making the gift fail the benefit test.

Again, it is clear that careful planning is needed. If the benefit had been expressed as the right to a discount on six tickets purchased over a year, then annualisation could not apply and the issue would have come down to a question of valuation of the right to receive the discount.

EXAMPLE 4.6

Miss Tomkins makes monthly payments of £20 to a charity under an open-ended standing order, in consequence of which she receives a free monthly magazine worth £2.50. Consider the categories:

4.28   Gift Aid – the Problem of Donor Benefit

Category	Gift	Benefit	Example
1	Single	Several received over interval of less than 12 months	Not applicable – series of gifts
2	Single	Single but related to period of less than 12 months	Not applicable – series of benefits and gifts
3	Series over less than 12 months	Series at intervals	Applicable – series of gifts and benefits
4	Series over less than 12 months	Single benefit	Not applicable – series of benefits

Annualisation applies and both benefit and gift are annualised by multiplying by 12. The donation becomes £240 and the benefit £30 – again, the relevant value test is failed.

It would seem possible that if Miss Tomkins had agreed to make an annual payment of £240 in 12 instalments that would have to be regarded as a single gift and annualisation would not apply and the gift would have qualified.

EXAMPLE 4.7

Mr Wong makes monthly payments of £2 a month to a charity under an open-ended standing order. In consequence of starting the payments he receives a one-off benefit of a pen worth £5. Applying the categories:

Category	Gift	Benefit	Example
1	Single	Several received over interval of less than 12 months	Not applicable – series of gifts and single benefit
2	Single	Single but related to period of less than 12 months	Not applicable – series of gifts and single benefit
3	Series over less than 12 months	Series at intervals	Not applicable – series of gifts but single benefit
4	Series over less than 12 months	Single benefit	Applicable – series of gifts but single benefit

Annualisation applies, but this time it is under *Finance Act 1990, s 25(5C)* not under *subsection (5B)* and is only applicable to the gift not the benefit. The gift is annualised by multiplying it by 12 making its value £24. The relevant amount is therefore 25% of this figure, ie £6, so the benefit of £5 is acceptable and the payment qualifies under Gift Aid.

PRACTICALITIES

4.29 The introduction of annualisation will make charities think carefully about both the payment arrangements for gifts and how they identify the benefits which might be applicable. It is likely to be most relevant in the case of subscriptions, but can also be a potential problem in situations where regular committed giving is encouraged by some token of appreciation.

Impact of overall limit

4.30 It is not sufficient for a benefit to satisfy the relevant value test in connection with the donation, it must also satisfy what the Inland Revenue refers to as the 'aggregate value test'. This test arises as a result of three existing subsections in the *Finance Act 1990, s 25*, and is further clarified by a phrase in *subsection (5D)*.

Finance Act 1990, s 25(2)(e) provides that the maximum amount of a benefit which can be taken into account in considering whether the donation remains valid should be £250. This is, therefore, the overriding limit. Obviously, where there is a single donation in excess of £10,000, the overriding figure of £250 will effectively replace the 2.5% limit as the relevant maximum.

Finance Act 1990, s 25(4)(b) applies the maximum figure of £250 where there is more than one benefit. The subsection states that the relevant value is to be:

> … where there is more than one benefit received in consequence of making it which is received by the donor or a person connected with him, the aggregate value of all the benefits received in consequence of making it which are received by the donor or a person connected with him.

Finance Act 1990, s 25(5) makes it clear that the amount which is to be compared to the limits set out in *subsection (2)(e)* is to be the aggregate of:

(a)   the relevant value in relation to the gift; and

(b)   the relevant value in relation to each gift already made to the charity by the donor in the relevant year of assessment which is a qualifying donation for the purposes of this section.

Benefits which arise as a result of donations which fail the relevant value test are not therefore to be aggregated and will not count towards the £250, thus avoiding a double penalty.

The final point of clarification comes at the end of *subsection (5D)* which states in unintelligible language that:

> … the reference in *subsection (5B)* above to *subsection (4)* above is a reference to that subsection as it applies for the purposes of *subsection (2)(e)* above.

Translating that into normal language, it says that in determining the aggregate value test it is necessary to take the actual value of the benefits received and not the annualised figure. This interpretation is confirmed by the Inland Revenue Guidance Notes.

How does the test work in practice? It is a case of looking at each gift and benefit arising to see if the specific rules apply to that donation but, at the same time, keep an eye on the total value of benefits that might be building up in the tax year.

EXAMPLE 4.8

Take the position of Ms Smith as set out at **Example 4.2** above. At February 2004 she had made total donations of £145 and received benefits of £30. The actual qualifying donations only amounted to the aggregate of the first three donations of £65, because the fourth payment of £80 was disqualified by the benefit. She makes two further donations in the tax year.

11 March 2004: she donates £9,600 in a charity auction and receives a weekend break actually worth £225. The value of the benefit has to be compared to the relevant value limit of 2.5% of the donation, ie £240, so it will qualify under that test. There are no other benefits with which to aggregate it and so the aggregate value test is also satisfied because that value remains under £250.

4 April 2004: she pays £4,000 for a dinner for two worth £90. This donation will again pass the relevant value test because that will be a maximum of 2.5% of £4,000 or £100. However, the value of the benefit of £90 must be aggregated with the benefit in connection with the weekend break and the combined total of £315 clearly exceeds the aggregate value of £250. The final donation therefore fails to qualify but the earlier donations are unaffected.

She would, of course, have been better advised to delay the final donation for just two days so that it fell into the next tax year!

Splitting the payments – a potential solution

4.31 Where a donation is clearly intertwined with a benefit in something like a theatre ticket or a charity dinner, there is a high risk that the donation may be ruled out under the relevant value test. The Inland Revenue is prepared to accept an alternative route which may preserve some of the qualifying nature of the payment. Effectively, the donor splits the sum he or she pays between a payment for the cost of the benefit he or she will receive and a pure donation. The latter will then qualify as a Gift Aid donation assuming, of course, all other relevant conditions are met.

EXAMPLE 4.9

In **Example 4.8** above, Ms Smith decides that she will pay the charity £90 for the dinner for two and will make a clear donation of £3,910. By doing this she avoids the aggregation of the benefit and is able to make the £3,910 a qualifying donation from which the charity will receive a further £1,112 in tax repayment.

PRACTICALITIES

4.32 Charities who want to go down this route for major fundraising events such as dinners or initiatives which offer free tickets for concerts, should make this option of a split arrangement very clear in the promotional literature for the event. The sums received from donors should then either be received as two distinct payments or should be accompanied by a letter or form which leaves no doubt that the benefit is being directly paid for. Obviously there must be some facility to actually make a Gift Aid declaration.

It has been possible in one situation to achieve this result retrospectively but this involved the charity in the exercise of contacting all donors and asking them if they were prepared to make a further payment for the benefit they expected to receive (free tickets). It also involved an appeal to the generous side of the Inland Revenue which, on this occasion, was thankfully in evidence.

Chapter 5   Gifts of Quoted Shares and Land

Introduction

5.1   At the start of **Chapter 2** in considering Gift Aid, mention was made of the original debate back in 1990 where it was supposedly made clear that Gift Aid would apply to gifts of money only. This was seen by many as a restriction because it prevented people who had assets, but not sufficient income to make tax-efficient gifts to charity. They might be able to sell the asset and then give the proceeds to charity, but even that may not have worked for Gift Aid if the donor did not have sufficient income chargeable to tax to cover the gift.

These issues were raised in the course of the Charities Tax Review at the end of the 1990s and in the legislation which followed that review in the *Finance Act 2000*, two provisions were introduced to make it easier for the asset rich/income poor to make donations. The first was the extension of Gift Aid itself to allow capital gains tax paid to cover the tax on the gift. The second was the introduction of a specific tax relief on donations of certain types of shares and securities.

In a surprise move, the relief was widened in the *Finance Act 2002* to cover gifts of land to charity. It had been thought that comments made at the time of the Charity Tax Review about difficulties of valuation of assets would have made any extension unlikely. Values of quoted shares are, of course, set independently by the market and are readily available in published market lists. Values of land are much more problematic and time will tell how the Inland Revenue is going to react to the process of establishing values in these cases. One can speculate that if there are no significant problems encountered, there is no logical reason why the relief should not be extended to other assets, such as works of art.

The reliefs are still very new and many donors are not aware of their potential. There are a number of practical issues which will be considered in this chapter.

● How does the relief work in practice?

● What shares qualify?

● How does one make the transfer?

● How does one calculate the value of the transfer?

● What land qualifies?

● What restrictions apply to land transactions?

● How is tax relief claimed by the donor?

● What is the position of the charity once it has received the shares?

● What is the position of the charity once it has received the land?

How does the relief work in practice?

Basic income tax relief

5.2   The basic relief is given by the *Income and Corporation Taxes Act 1988, s 587B* and applies where an individual or a company passes a holding of quoted shares or a qualifying interest in land to a charity either as a gift or at a value below the then market value. The relief centres on what the legislation calls the 'relevant amount', which is either:

● the full market value of the asset transferred (where the transfer is a gift);

● the difference between the market value and the actual cash received (where transfer is a sale at undervalue).

This figure is then adjusted by adding to it the incidental costs of disposing of the asset and by reducing it by the value of any benefit which the donor may receive from the charity in return for the donation. For example, if a parent made a transfer of shares to a school in return for reduced fees for their child who attended the school, the value of the saving on the fees would be deducted in calculating the 'relevant value'.

Where an individual makes the transfer, they will be able to deduct the 'relevant amount' from their total income for income tax purposes and so will make a tax saving. Where the transferor is a company, the relevant value will be treated as a charge and deducted from its profits for corporation tax purposes.

EXAMPLE 5.1

Henry, who has an annual income of £100,000, gifts quoted shares to the value of £20,000 to a charity. The shares originally cost £5,000 (ignoring costs).

Henry can claim that for income tax purposes his income will be reduced by £20,000, which at an effective tax rate of 40% would amount to relief of £8,000.

EXAMPLE 5.2

The basic facts are as above except that the shares are owned by Henry Ltd. The company is chargeable to corporation tax at the small companies rate of 19% on its profits, its taxable profits would be reduced by £20,000, a relief in tax terms of £3,800.

The following two examples taken from the Inland Revenue website show how the 'relevant amount' is to be calculated.

EXAMPLE 5.3

Angela owns 5,000 shares in ABC plc, a company quoted on the London Stock Exchange. The shares are given to a charity when they are worth £10 each. A broker's fee of £50 is charged for handling the transaction. As a token of gratitude the charity gives Angela tickets to an event worth £500.

The deduction that Angela can make is:

the value of the shares:	£50,000
plus the broker's fee:	£50
	£50,050
less the value of the benefit received	£500
	£49,550

EXAMPLE 5.4

John owns 1,000 shares in XYZ plc, a company quoted on the London Stock Exchange. The shares are valued at £4.50 each. He would like to give the shares to a charity, but needs to realise some money from them. So, he agrees to sell them to the charity for £2 each. As a token of gratitude the charity gives him a book worth £25.

The deduction that the John can make is:

the value of the shares	£4,500
less the amount the charity pays	£2,000
	£2,500
less the value of the benefit received	£25
	£2,475

Anti-avoidance legislation

5.3   As so often happens with tax 'breaks', the tax-avoidance industry quickly gets to work to find ways in which the tax break can be used by those who have high tax liability. Schemes were devised which effectively gave the donor of the shares the full deduction for the value transferred to the charity, but a series of devices meant that the charity only received a fraction of that figure. Legislation was introduced in the *Finance Act 2004* to counter this. The effect of the Act's provisions is to ensure that if the benefit to the charity is limited then the donor will only receive tax relief on the benefit that the charity receives.

What about capital gains?

5.4   There was no change made to the capital gains tax (CGT) rules on a donation of assets to a charity. The legislation in the *Taxation of Chargeable Gains Act 1992, s 257 (TCGA 1992)* provides that:

5.4 Gifts of Quoted Shares and Land

(1) *Subsection (2)* below shall apply where a disposal of an asset is made otherwise than under a bargain at arm's length—

(a) to a charity; or

(b) to any bodies mentioned in *Schedule 3* to the *Inheritance Tax Act 1984* (gifts for national purposes, etc),

and the disposal is not one in relation to which *section 151A(1)* has effect.

(2) *Sections 17(1)* and *258(3)* shall not apply; but if the disposal is by way of gift (including a gift in settlement) or for a consideration not exceeding the sums allowable as a deduction under *section 38*, then—

(a) the disposal and acquisition shall be treated for the purposes of this Act as being made for such consideration as to secure that neither a gain nor a loss accrues on the disposal; and

(b) where, after the disposal, the asset is disposed of by the person who acquired it under the disposal, its acquisition by the person making the earlier disposal shall be treated for the purposes of this Act as the acquisition of the person making the later disposal.

The section also deals with a situation where an asset is held in a trust and a charity becomes a beneficiary under the terms of the trust.

The relief applies not only to transfers to UK charities, but also covers transfers to a range of other bodies which are listed in the inheritance tax legislation. A number of these are charities in their own right. The full list is comprised as follows.

- The National Gallery.

- The British Museum.

- The National Museums of Scotland.

- The National Museum of Wales.

- The Ulster Museum.

- Any other similar national institution which exists wholly or mainly for the purpose of preserving for the public benefit a collection of scientific, historic or artistic interest and which is approved for the purposes of this Schedule by the Treasury.

- Any museum or art gallery in the United Kingdom which exists wholly or mainly for that purpose and is maintained by a local authority or university in the United Kingdom.

- Any library the main function of which is to serve the needs of teaching and research at a university in the United Kingdom.

- The Historic Buildings and Monuments Commission for England.

- The National Trust for Places of Historic Interest or Natural Beauty.

- The National Trust for Scotland for Places of Historic Interest or Natural Beauty.
- The National Art Collections Fund.
- The Trustees of the National Heritage Memorial Fund.
- The National Endowment for Science, Technology and the Arts.
- The Friends of the National Libraries.
- The Historic Churches Preservation Trust.
- Nature Conservancy Council for England.
- Scottish Natural Heritage.
- Countryside Council for Wales.
- Any local authority.
- Any Government department (including the National Debt Commissioners).
- Any university or university college in the United Kingdom.
- A health service body, within the meaning of *section 519A* of the *Income and Corporation Taxes Act 1988*.

So the basic principle is that on a transfer to a charity, the transferor must consider the capital gains situation and calculate the value which will give the transferor neither a gain nor a loss on the transfer. This will mean taking into account:

(a) the original cost of the assets;

(b) any indexation on the cost (for individuals this will be indexation up to 5 April 1998 but for companies, indexation still applies to gains); and

(c) any incidental costs of acquisition.

This figure is needed to give the starting cost of the asset for the charity.

EXAMPLE 5.5

Going back to the facts in **Example 5.1** where Henry had gifted shares to the value of £20,000 to charity – those shares had an original cost of £5,000 and the CGT position will therefore be that Henry will have made a disposal at a value of £5,000 and this will be the cost which the charity will use in any subsequent disposal.

Is this a better option than selling the asset and making a gift?

5.5   There is no easy answer to the question. It depends on particular circumstances and whether an individual donor wants to retain tax relief or allow the charity to benefit. A donation of shares gives the charity the value of the shares, whereas a payment under Gift Aid allows the charity a greater receipt.

5.5 Gifts of Quoted Shares and Land

EXAMPLE 5.6

Wendy pays income tax at the higher rate. She has shares worth £100,000 and is considering a donation of that sum to a charity. If she were to sell the shares she would have a capital gain, after taper relief and annual allowance of £20,000.

She sells the shares and donates net of tax proceeds under Gift Aid:

Gross proceeds from sale of shares	£100,000
Less CGT (20,000 × 40%)	£8,000
Net proceeds after tax	£92,000
Gift Aid donation net	£92,000
Grossing up for charity	£25,948
Gross value of gift to charity	**£117,948**
Additional higher-rate relief for Wendy (18%)	£21,230
The gift has cost Wendy 100,000 – 21,230	**£78,770**
Gifts the shares directly to the charity	
Charity receives	**£100,000**
Wendy has tax relief of £100,000 × 40% £40,000	
Cost of Gift to Wendy is	**£60,000**

In the case of a corporate donor, the answer is more straightforward. The company makes a Gift Aid payment gross and would get no further relief. If it had to pay corporation tax on any capital gain that would make the gift of shares route attractive.

EXAMPLE 5.7

The facts are as for **Example 5.6** except that the shares are owned by Wendy Ltd, a company that pays CT at the small companies rate of 19%.

The company sells the shares and donates net of tax proceeds under Gift Aid:

Gross proceeds from sale of shares	£100,000
Less CGT (20,000 × 19%)	£3,800
Net proceeds after tax	£96,200
Gift Aid donation (gross)	£96,200
Grossing up for charity	nil
Gross value of gift to charity	**£96,200**
CT relief on gift (96,200 × 19%)	£18,278
The gift has cost Wendy Ltd 100,000 – 18,278	**£81,722**
Gifts the shares directly to the charity	
Charity receives	**£100,000**
Wendy Ltd has tax relief of £100,000 × 19%	£19,000
Cost of Gift to Wendy Ltd is	**£81,000**

What shares qualify?

5.6   The legislation states that the qualifying shares must be within the following categories:

- shares and securities listed or dealt in on a UK stock exchange including the Alternative Investment Market (AIM);

- shares and securities listed or dealt in on recognised foreign stock exchanges;

- units in an authorised unit trust;

- shares in a UK open-ended investment company (OEIC);

- holdings in certain foreign collective investment schemes – broadly equivalent to UK unit trusts or OEICs.

Recognised stock exchanges

5.7   The Inland Revenue publishes lists of recognised stock exchanges. These are recognised within the *Income and Corporation Taxes Act 1988, s 841* and currently comprise the following:

- Athens Stock Exchange;

- Australian Stock Exchange and any subsidiaries;

- Colombo Stock Exchange;

- Helsinki Stock Exchange;

- Johannesburg Stock Exchange;

- Korea Stock Exchange;

- Kuala Lumpur Stock Exchange;

- Mexico Stock Exchange;

- New Zealand Stock Exchange;

- Rio de Janeiro Stock Exchange;

- Sao Paulo Stock Exchange;

- Singapore Stock Exchange;

- Stockholm Stock Exchange;

- Stock Exchange of Thailand;

- Swiss Stock Exchange.

In addition, any stock exchange in the following countries which is a stock exchange within the meaning of the laws of that country:

- Austria;

- Belgium (including EASDAQ);

- Canada (any stock exchange prescribed for purposes of Canadian Income Tax Act);

- France;

- Germany;

- Hong Kong (any stock exchange recognised under s 2A of Hong Kong Companies Ordinance);

- Italy;

- Ireland;

- Japan;

- Luxembourg;

- Netherlands;

- Norway;

- Portugal;

- Spain;

- USA – any stock exchange registered with the Securities and Exchange Commission as a national securities exchange;

- USA – the NASDAQ Stock Market as maintained through the facilities of the National Association Of Securities Dealers Inc and its subsidiaries.

How is the transfer of shares made?

5.8   If an individual wants to make a donation of qualifying shares, the first step should be to contact the charity and ask if it can accept such a gift. Not every charity will have the power to accept and hold such an investment under the terms of its founding document, or it may not believe it within its code of beliefs to accept shares or a particular type of share – an extreme example would be a health charity being asked to receive shares in a tobacco company.

Once it is clear that the charity will accept the shares, the donor needs to contact the share registrar for the company to obtain a share transfer form. The name of the registrar should be on the share certificate or other documentation. Large companies rarely do their own share registration preferring to leave the job to large specialist organisations. If there is no obvious information about the registrar, a call to the company should elicit the information.

Charities need to make sure that they have someone in their organisation who understands the share transfer procedure so that they can deal with potential queries on the mechanics.

Some people may consider that their small shareholdings may not be of interest to charities. There is an organisation called Sharegift which operates as a conduit for share donations to charity. It will help with the paperwork and can consolidate small donations into larger amounts to go to charities. Further information can be obtained from Sharegift, 46 Grosvenor Street, London, W1K 3HN, telephone 020 7337 0501, website: www.sharegift.org

The Charities Aid Foundation also offer a facility for people to make transfers of shares to them either to hold in one of their accounts pending a decision on the end recipient, or to direct the sale proceeds to go to a specific charity.

How is the value of the transfer of shares calculated?

5.9   The tax relief is based on the market value of the shares or securities on the day on which they were transferred. This will usually be the date on which the share transfer document was signed. The Inland Revenue publishes the following guidance on how to establish the correct value:

> Shares or securities quoted in the London Stock Exchange Daily Official List.

> You should use either:

> ● the lower of the two quotations on the day in question plus one quarter of the difference between those two amounts; or

> ● the mid point between the highest and lowest prices on which bargains were done on the day, except for bargains at special prices,

> whichever is the lower.

> Bargains at special prices are clearly shown in the Daily Official List. They should not be included in the comparison of highest and lowest prices. Bargains at special prices are now very rare.

> For other shares or securities listed or dealt in on a recognised stock exchange, there is no special formula for valuing these. Their market value is the price which those assets might reasonably be expected to fetch on a sale in the open market.

> Where shares are quoted on an overseas stock exchange it will normally be acceptable to take the value as the price quoted on that exchange for the day of the gift, translated into sterling at the rate of exchange for that day.

> Prices for these shares and securities and those quoted in the London Stock Exchange Daily Official List are often published in the financial pages of newspapers. The newspaper valuations may be used where the parcel of shares is modest.

> **Units in UK Authorised Unit Trusts (AUTs)**

> You should use the selling price (also called the 'bid price' the price at which units are sold by investors) published by the unit trust manager for the day in question. The 'selling price' is usually given in the financial

pages of newspapers under 'authorised investment funds'. If no price was published for the day in question you should use the last price published before that day.

Shares in UK Open Ended Investment Companies (OEICs)

You should use the published price for the day in question. This can usually be found in the financial pages of newspapers under 'authorised investment funds'. If no price was published for the day in question you should use the last price published before that day.

Holdings in foreign collective investment schemes

You should use the published price for the day in question. This can usually be found in the financial pages of newspapers under 'offshore or overseas funds'. If no price was published for the day in question you should use the last price published before that day or contact the fund manager.

What land qualifies?

5.10 The legislation in the *Finance Act 2002* introduces a fifth class of 'qualifying investment' into the *Income and Corporation Taxes Act 1988, s 587B(9)* (*ICTA 1988*) and terms it 'a qualifying interest in land'. This is defined in *subsection (9A)* as:

(a) a freehold interest in land; or

(b) a leasehold interest in land which is a term of years absolute where the land in question is in the United Kingdom.

The inference from the reference to the UK in (b) is that the freehold land can be anywhere in the world. The relief applies for transfers made by an individual after 6 April 2002 and by a company after 1 April 2002.

The transfer must be of the whole interest in the land. It is not possible to give away a part of an interest. It is also not possible for a person to give away the land but retain some rights in it.

EXAMPLE 5.8

Eric owns the freehold of a property which he rents out. He would like to donate a 50% interest in the property to a local charity so that it can benefit from some of the income and also the capital growth in the value of the property. He can, of course, do this, but he will not be able to claim any income tax relief in respect of the donation.

EXAMPLE 5.9

Ernie owns his own house and wants to transfer it to charity now. He has no immediate beneficiaries and although the transfer will be exempt from IHT if he leaves the property to the charity in his will, Ernie has considerable income from the successful plays he has written and he would like to have the income tax relief now. If he makes a gift but retains a right to live in the property rent-free for the rest of his life that will not work.

There are two further clarifications of the definition. *ICTA 1988, s 587B(9D)* makes clear that an agreement to acquire a freehold interest and an agreement to acquire a leasehold interest are not qualifying interests in land. *ICTA 1988, s 587B(9E)* makes clear that for Scotland:

(a) references to a freehold interest in land are references to the interests of the owner; and

(b) references to a leasehold interest in land which is a term of years absolute are references to the interest of a tenant in the property subject to lease.

Grant of a lease

5.11 Where a lease is granted either out of a freehold or a leasehold interest and that lease is gifted to a charity that will be regarded for the purposes of *ICTA 1988, s 587B* as a disposal of the whole beneficial interest in the qualifying investment (*s 587B(9C)*). This will prevent relief being claimed on a creation of the lease and then again on a subsequent transfer of the superior interest.

EXAMPLE 5.10

Hector owns a freehold property comprising a small office building. He decides to let the offices to a firm of accountants at a commercial rental. The lease is for 25 years. He then gifts the lease to a charity so that it can receive the rental. Hector will be regarded as making a gift for the purposes of *ICTA 1988, s 587B*. Ten years later, Hector decides to transfer the freehold to the same charity. The two interests will then merge. Although Hector has now made a complete disposal of his interest in the property to the charity, he will not be able to make a further claim under *s 587B*.

Joint ownership

5.12 Where two or more persons have a qualifying interest in land, either as joint tenants or tenants in common, *ICTA 1988, s 587B* can only apply if all the individuals make the gift to the charity (*s 587C(2)*). The amount of relief available to each individual is to be such share of the relevant amount as is agreed between the individuals (*s 587C(3)*). This limits the relief in aggregate to the relevant amount but does seem to allow some measure of flexibility in determining how much relief each individual should have. This could be relevant if spouses make the gift and one spouse is a taxpayer and the other not. Presumably, a claim can be made by the taxpayer spouse in respect of the entire relevant amount if needed.

EXAMPLE 5.11

Margo and Gerry own a residential property as tenants in common. The actual share is 75% Margo and 25% for Gerry because Gerry is a higher-rate taxpayer and Margo is not, and the couple have elected under *ICTA 1988, s 282* for the income to be taxed in that ratio to minimise their liability. The election under *ICTA 1988, s 587B* must be made by them both, but it seems possible for them to agree a ratio which is different to the one they use for income tax purposes, so that the majority of the relief can be given to Gerry.

Certificate to be issued by the charity

5.13 A certificate must be given by or on behalf of the charity before a claim can be admitted (*ICTA 1988, s 587C(4)*). The claim has to specify the description of the qualifying interest in land which is the subject of the disposal, specify the date of the disposal and contain a statement that the charity has acquired the qualifying interest (*s 587C(5)*). There is no official form of the certificate and the charity can put this in whatever format they wish.

Withdrawal of relief

5.14 Relief given under *ICTA 1988, s 587B* will be withdrawn by assessment if within a certain period (known as the relevant period), the person making the gift or any person connected with them either becomes entitled to an interest or right in relation to all or part of the land or becomes a party to an arrangement under which he enjoys some right in relation to all or part of the land, otherwise than for full consideration in money or money's worth. The only exception is where those rights are obtained as a result of a disposition of property on death. The relevant period for an individual is the fifth anniversary of 31 January next following the end of the year of assessment in which the original disposal was made. For a company, it will be six years from the end of the accounting period in which the transfer was made (*s 587C(6)–(11)*).

EXAMPLE 5.12

John Brown makes a gift of a commercial property comprising a shop and flat to a charity in December 2003 and claims relief under *ICTA 1988, s 587B*. In June 2005, John's son, Bill, is given a lease to occupy the flat by the charity. This will be a disqualifying event and since it occurs within the relevant period, the relief that John originally received will be removed.

How is tax relief claimed by the donor?

5.15 Relief can be claimed primarily through the appropriate section of the self-assessment tax return. The 2004 return contains a box at 15A.6 for making a claim in respect of shares. In the calculation of tax liability, the market value of the shares should be deducted from the gross income for the year before personal allowances.

Those in employment could ask for their coding for the year to be adjusted to take account of the relief. This should be shown as an addition to the allowances side of the code and when the revised code is implemented, the full tax relief should be given.

It might be that the donation will impact on the payments on account due under the self-assessment regime and a claim can be made to reduce those payments on account. Care should be taken before doing this in case there are any other factors known for the year which might impact in such a way as to leave the amount of the payments unchanged.

It is important to retain some record of the transfer since this forms part of the supporting documentation and could be requested by the Inland Revenue. A copy of the share transfer form should be retained together with any correspondence with the charity about the gift.It is also important to keep evidence to show how the value of the shares was arrived at.

What is the position of the charity?

What does the charity do with the shares?

5.16 What the charity does with the shares is up to the charity. Some charities have an investment portfolio and the donated shares might be added to that and dealt with in accordance with the investment policy of the charity. For some charities, the investments, although welcomed as additional resources, need to be turned into cash at the earliest possible time, and the charity will therefore sell the shares.

Basic exemption for CGT

5.17 The basic CGT exemption for charities is in the *Taxation of Chargeable Gains Act 1992, s 256*, which sets out the basic exemption as follows:

> '(1) Subject to *section 505(3)* of the *Taxes Act* and *subsection (2)* below, a gain shall not be a chargeable gain if it accrues to a charity and is applicable and applied for charitable purposes.

Note that the exemption applies only where the gain is applicable and applied for charitable purposes which mirrors the income tax exemption. It is, however, only the gain which has to be so applied and not the total proceeds.

Provided that charities are sensible in their planning on disposal of chargeable assets, there should be no tax problems as long as the charity remains in existence.

Chapter 6   Making a Legacy to Charity

Introduction

Importance of legacies

6.1   Many charities receive a significant proportion of their income via legacies, and most charities see the importance of legacies as part of their fundraising portfolio. A search on the Internet using the words 'legacy and charity' brings up the websites of most charities. Some have really geared themselves up to promote and handle legacies. Some even offer a will-writing service with no tie-in. Legacies can come in very variable amounts and not all are received in monetary form with gifts of property and assets being provided as well.

Inheritance tax (IHT) background

6.2   The primary attraction of legacies from a tax point of view is that they are free of inheritance tax (IHT). This tax was introduced by the *Finance Act 1986* to replace capital transfer tax which had, itself, replaced Estate Duty in the *Finance Act 1975*. The introduction of Capital Transfer Tax (CTT) had been intended to curb the practice of giving away assets before death by imposing a tax, albeit at a lower rate, when the gift was made. IHT is, in many ways, a hybrid of its two predecessors. Some gifts can now escape the charge to tax provided that they are made more than seven years before death.

Some transfers, known as potentially exempt transfers, bear no charge to tax at the time they are made but become chargeable if the donor dies within seven years of making the gift. Other transfers are chargeable to tax at the time they are made with a possible further charge to tax if the death of the donor occurs within seven years.

The basic principle of the tax is that it is levied on the reduction in the value of the estate of an individual which occurs as a result of his transferring an asset out of that estate. The legislation refers to this as a 'transfer of value'. The straightforward gift of an asset is within the definition, as are some less obvious dispositions such as the failure to exercise a right or the sale of an asset at undervalue, both of which can be said to reduce the size of the estate.

On death, the individual is deemed to have disposed of his or her entire estate and the tax is therefore levied on the value of the assets in the estate at the date of death.

EXEMPTIONS

6.3   A number of exemptions are available, the most common of which is the annual exemption of £3,000. This can be carried forward for one year giving a maximum exemption of £6,000. Other exemptions include gifts to a spouse, gifts up to £250 to any individual in any year, gifts in consideration of marriage and gifts out of income.

TAX RATES

6.4   Unlike other taxes which operate on a fiscal year basis with new limits and rate bands applying each year, IHT operates on a cumulative basis with the value of chargeable transfers being added together and the appropriate and, usually, higher rate of tax applying to each successive transfer. Chargeable transfers are accumulated only with those made in the previous seven years.

The actual rates of tax begin with a nil-rate band, which for 2004/05 runs to £263,000 and is index-linked. Thereafter there is one rate of 40%. The rate of tax on chargeable transfers made during a lifetime is at half the main rate but can be increased if death occurs within a seven-year period.

The IHT provisions only apply directly to charities in certain situations which are discussed below. An understanding of the basic provisions of IHT is, however, essential to charities in that they have a considerable impact on two major sources of income for charities, gifts and legacies. Whilst the exemption is generous there are some pitfalls and these are also considered below.

Practical issues

6.5   The major practical issue is to ensure that the terms of the will are clear as to which assets are to pass to charity and in what way. There are a number of ways in which assets can actually be left, and some of these are not as tax efficient as others. The primary way will be an absolute gift to charity, but sometimes people choose to leave assets in the form of trusts and can give different types of interest in those trusts. It would be helpful to identify some of the jargon that is used in this context.

Term	Definition
Settlement	This covers any situation where someone makes assets available to others in such a way that they confer a bounteous gift on them.
Trust	A legal document that is a type of settlement.
Settlor	The person who donates the capital that creates the settlement.
Trustees	The individuals (or, in some cases, a corporate body) who have legal responsibility for all the assets held in the trust. This can include the settlor (obviously not in the case of a will trust) and can also include people who are beneficiaries.
Executors	The individuals (or corporate trustee) responsible for the administration of the will of a deceased.

Term	Definition
Beneficiary	An individual or a body such as a charity which is to receive a benefit under the terms of the trust deed. The nature of their interest will be specified in the deed.
Trust income	The income that arises to the trustees as a result of assets invested. The income may be accumulated and held within the trust or it may be paid out (distributed) to beneficiaries in accordance with the trust deed.
Trust capital	This will usually be the original capital put into the trust on its creation or added to the trust by the original settlor. The terms of the trust may specifiy that the capital has to remain in the trust – this may be referred to sometimes as an 'endowment'. The deed may allow trust capital to be passed to beneficiaries.
Absolute interest	This arises when the trust effectively passes ownership of trust assets to beneficiaries. The technical ownership, eg registration of shares may be in the name of the trustees but in reality the trustees have no control over what happens to the assets.
Interest in possession	Defined as being the 'present right to present enjoyment' of the assets. Will arise if an individual has the right to receive some or all of the trust income each year. Could also arise if a beneficiary has the right to occupy a trust property rent-free. Sometimes known as a 'life interest' and the person who holds it is referred to as the 'life tenant' (in Scotland the 'life renter').
Discretionary benefit	This is a benefit that is held at the discretion of the trustees. They decide which beneficiaries, if any, are to receive trust income and/or capital.
Defeasible or revocable interest	This is an interest in possession that can be revoked by the trustees under powers contained in the trust deed.
Contingent interest	This is an interest that arises only when a contingency is satisfied. For example, a child might have an interest that depends upon them reaching the age of 18 – that will be a contingent interest.
Reversionary interest	When a life interest comes to an end, for example, when the life tenant dies. The assets will then 'revert' to someone else at that time.
Instrument of variation	A legal arrangement which can be used to modify the direction of legacies. Beneficiaries can agree on a different distribution and this is treated as if the deceased made the distribution. Must be completed within two years of the death and the Inland Revenue must be advised.

Inheritance tax and legacies to charity

Gifts to charities – basic exemption

6.6   Specific exemption is given by the *Inheritance Tax Act 1984, s 23(1)* (*IHTA 1984*) for transfers of value to the extent that the 'values transferred by them are attributable to property which is given to charities'. For clarification, *IHTA 1984, s 23(6)* provides that a property is given to charity 'if it becomes the property of charitable purposes only'.

The above exemption applies to both lifetime transfers and transfers on death by an individual. It also applies where assets are transferred into a trust to be held for charitable purposes only. There is no financial limit to the exemption, so in simple terms, if an individual left all of his or her estate to charity there would be no IHT liability at all. Any legacy to a charity would be deducted from the value of the estate before the IHT liability was calculated.

MEANING OF CHARITY

6.7   The terms 'charity' and 'charitable' are defined in the *IHTA 1984, s 272* as having the same meaning as for income tax purposes. The basic income tax definition is 'a body established for charitable purposes' and this has been held in the courts to mean:

- the charity must be established in the United Kingdom; and

- the term must have the same meaning in Scotland as in England.

Therefore, a legacy to a charity in France or the United States would not qualify for exemption. There are two further practical points to bear in mind:

- a gift to a needy individual, even if made for sound charitable reasons, will not meet the definition of being for charitable purposes; and

- a gift described as being for 'benevolent' purposes, will not qualify because benevolence goes beyond the meaning of charity in law.

RELEVANT DATE FOR CHARITABLE STATUS

6.8   The basic rule is that the beneficiary must be charitable at the time the assets are transferred to it. There are two sets of circumstances in which the Inland Revenue will accept that a body which acquires charitable status after the gift can benefit from the exemption. These are:

- a trust created under the Will of the deceased; and

- a situation where a beneficiary under a will enters into an instrument of variation and redirects some of his or her legacy to a charity.

EXAMPLE 6.1

Edith died in July 2004 and left a legacy to the local family history society. At the time of her death, the society is not a registered charity and the legacy will not be exempt. However, in October 2005, James, the main beneficiary under the will makes an instrument of variation which confers a benefit on the society which has now become a charity. The exemption will then apply.

IDENTIFY THE BENEFICIARY

6.9   It is very important to specify the beneficiary very clearly and carefully and to ensure that the beneficiary will meet the requirements for the IHT exemption. The Inland Revenue Capital Taxes Office (CTO) instructions tell the examiners who review IHT accounts to check very carefully who the precise beneficiary is. In particular, they are told to identify:

(a)   situations where there may be related organisations with similar names, one of which is a UK charity and one of which is not;

(b)   where the legacy is paid for the work of an individual who is known for charitable work (the Inland Revenue example which is now out of date is Mother Theresa);

(c)   whether the gift is subject to any trusts and the terms of those trusts;

(d)   if the name of the charity has been incorrectly recorded in the will;

(e)   if the charity has changed its name since the will was written.

The examiners are told to read very carefully the clauses in the will giving the charitable legacy and it will be sensible for those drafting the will in the first place to make sure that the wording will ensure that there will be charitable exemption for the legacy.

Executors who find themselves faced with a wording of a legacy that falls under (a) or (b) above, may decide to pay the legacy to a related qualifying body or charity instead of to the beneficiary named in the will. That will not work. Similarly, an individual, eg a church dignitary who has been left a legacy by a stranger may pass it on to a recognised charity – again that will not work. The only effective way of dealing with the matter is for an instrument of variation to be executed to substitute the intended beneficiary.

Inland Revenue examiners are told that where the terms of the will are clear they must be followed. Where the terms are not clear, eg where the name of the intended beneficiary has been misquoted or changed, some discretion may be exercised. The CTO manual gives a list of categories of organisations which may be usually accepted as being charitable provided certain conditions (which unhelpfully are not published) are satisfied. The categories are as follows:

(a)   Category 1:

   ●   cathedrals;

- diocesan Boards of Finance;
- church officers where the gift is for the upkeep of the church etc;
- parish churches which may also be minsters or abbeys;
- parochial church councils;
- churches of recognised denominations including chapels and mission halls;
- missionary societies;
- moral welfare associations;
- Sunday schools.

(b) Category 2:

- child welfare associations;
- children's homes;
- community centres;
- convalescent homes;
- homes for the blind;
- hospital homes;
- mentally handicapped groups;
- old people's welfare committees;
- orphanages;
- physically handicapped groups.

(c) Category 3:

- area health authorities;
- hospices;
- hospitals (including private hospitals);
- hospital management committees;
- leagues of friends of hospitals;
- medical research funds;
- nursing associations;
- patient amenity funds attached to hospitals;
- Samaritan funds attached to hospitals.

(d) Category 4:

Any branch of an organisation which is governed by Royal Charter and which is itself acceptable as charitable. Notable examples are:

- Boy Scouts;

- British Red Cross;

- Girl Guides;

- Royal British Legion (branches not clubs);

- St John Ambulance Brigade;

- Sea Cadet Corps.

In some situations the Inland Revenue may ask the executors to provide further extrinsic evidence that might help identify the beneficiary as a charitable body. Usually where the information is forthcoming and the amount of the legacy is under £10,000 the matter will be accepted and exemption given.

OBJECTS OUTSIDE THE UK

6.10 A number of UK registered charities have primary objects such as relief of poverty, which are fulfilled abroad. The gift will be accepted as being charitable even though the deceased may have specifically requested that it be earmarked for an overseas project, eg a gift to Oxfam for work in Africa.

GIFTS TO CONGLOMERATE CHARITIES

6.11 Some organisations, such as the Charities Aid Foundation (CAF), publicise the fact that they can act as a clearing house for charitable legacies. The deceased leaves the aggregate sum to CAF and, as a charity, that legacy should be exempt. The deceased may have left wishes as to how the sum should be allocated and these can be followed by the executors and further distributions made in due course from the CAF account. The Inland Revenue accepts that where a wish is made that will be no problem. It does state that where the bequest is accompanied by a direction that it should be applied for purposes outside the UK they will refuse the relief.

Restrictions of exemption

6.12 The apparent generosity of the legislators in providing exemption for charities is somewhat tempered by the fact that there are four subsections to *IHTA 1984, s 23* which restrict the basic exemption given in *section 23(1)*.

POSTPONED GIFTS

6.13 Where a disposition to a charity can only take effect after some other interest has terminated or a period of time has elapsed, then no exemption would be afforded to such a transfer. The Inland Revenue's view is that the phrase 'take effect' must mean 'takes effect in possession'. Therefore, if D dies leaving the residue of their estate to E for his life and then to charity, there will be no exemption on D's death, although it is likely that there would be an exemption on E's death (*IHTA 1984, s 23(2)(a)*).

CONDITIONAL GIFTS

6.14   *IHTA 1984, s 23(2)(b)* takes out of the exemption some gifts which are conditional. Where a gift is conditional on something happening and the condition is not met within a period of twelve months of the transfer, the gift will not be exempt. A charity faced with such a gift knowing that it would be impossible to fulfil the condition within the stated period would be advised to try to arrange for the sum involved to be made over as a loan and not as a transfer of value for IHT purposes until such time as the condition has been satisfied, at which point the loan could be written off and would be exempt as transfer of value under the *IHTA 1984, s 23(1)*.

DEFEASIBLE GIFTS

6.15   Where a gift can be retracted within a period of 12 months from the date on which it was made, no exemption is available. Where retraction does not take place in that period, exemption may be given provided no possibility remains that the gift may ever be retracted (*IHTA 1984, s 23(2)(c)*).

GIFT LESS THAN DONOR'S WHOLE INTEREST OR FOR A LIMITED PERIOD

6.16   Under *IHTA 1984 s 23(3)*, no exemption is provided where the gift represents an interest in other property (defined in its widest sense) and either of the two following situations arise:

(a)   the interest given is less than the donor's interest in the same property – a question of fact to be determined 12 months after the transfer. In such circumstances, the donor's retention of the superior interest would serve to make the gift capable of being rescinded. An example would be the creation of a leasehold interest for the charity with the freehold retained by the donor; or

(b)   the interest transferred is given only for a limited period.

INTEREST RESERVED OR CREATED

6.17   Where the property being transferred is land or a building, no exemption will be given if the donor reserves or creates an interest in the property which entitles him, his spouse or a person connected with him to occupy or possess the whole or part of the building either rent-free or for a less than commercial rent. This would cover the gifting of the freehold of a property where the donor reserved a leasehold interest to himself, which allowed him to remain in occupation of the property (*IHTA 1984, s 23(4)(a)*).

Similar provisions cover property other than land and buildings where the donor creates or reserves an interest in the property. The exemption would, however, be maintained if the interest was created for full consideration or the interest did not in any substantial way prevent the charity from enjoying the property (*IHTA 1984, s 23(4)(b)*).

GIFT NOT LIMITED TO CHARITABLE PURPOSES

6.18 The final restriction is found in *IHTA 1984, s 23(5)* which excludes gifts which may in whole or in part become applicable to non-charitable purposes. There are some circumstances in which a charity can apply the gift to strictly non-charitable purposes and they are:

(a) gifts to political parties (subject to the party having obtained the requisite Parliamentary representation) (*IHTA 1984, s 24*);

(b) gifts for national purposes as defined in *IHTA 1984, Sch 3* (*IHTA 1984, s 25*); and

(c) gifts for public benefit (*IHTA 1984, s 26*).

Gifts made direct to bodies within (a)–(c) above qualify for exemption from IHT in their own right, so that the proviso to *IHTA 1984, s 23(5)* merely extends that exemption to the situation where the donor effectively makes a gift via the charity.

Application of exemption to settled property

6.19 The exemption applies in a number of circumstances where property, which has been in a trust passes to a charity. For example:

- property left on trust for F in his lifetime and then to revert to charity. When F dies, the exemption will be available;

- property left to G for their life with remainder to H. Whilst G is still alive, H gives the reversion to charity. On G's death the charity exemption will be available.

Again there is a need for some care because the legislation does not allow the exemption in certain circumstances.

SETTLEMENT COMES TO AN END

6.20 The provisions of the *IHTA 1984, s 56(3)(a)* require the settlement to come to an end where an interest in possession comes to an end and the property reverts to a charity. Three examples are given in the Inland Revenue CTO manual:

- property given to I for life with the remainder to go as one-half to a charity absolutely and the other half to J for life. On I's death, the settlement will end as far as the half of the property given to charity is concerned and so the exemption applies;

- property given to K for life with remainder to L. On his deathbed, K makes a gift of the life interest to a charity. The exemption cannot apply because the settlement continues;

- property is given to M for his life with reversion to charity. M surrenders his life interest in favour of the charity. That brings the settlement to an end and the exemption will apply.

ACQUISITION OF REVERSION FROM A CHARITY

6.21 If property is given to a charity in exchange for a reversionary interest in a settlement, the exemption will not apply unless the reversionary interest forms part of the estate of the person acquiring it. This is to prevent avoidance.

PURCHASE OF A REVERSIONARY INTEREST BY A CHARITY

6.22 *IHTA 1984, s 56(3)(b)* operates to prevent the charity exemption in circumstances where:

- immediately before becoming the property of the charity or other exempt body it was comprised in a settlement; and

- an interest in the settlement is or has been acquired for a consideration in money or money's worth by that or another exempt body.

Inheritance tax and the charity

6.23 The previous section was concerned with the charity as the recipient of the gift. However, other provisions within the IHT legislation relate to charitable trusts and can, in some circumstances, trigger an IHT charge on the charity.

Discretionary trusts

6.24 Because of the possibilities which exist for individuals avoiding IHT by transferring assets into what are commonly referred to as discretionary trusts (in the Act 'settlements without interest in possession'), there are specific provisions for taxing the value of property in such trusts every ten years (commonly referred to as the 'ten-year charge'). Charitable trusts are effectively settlements in which there is no interest in possession and they would, therefore, be liable to the ten-year charge were it not for *IHTA 1984, s 58(1)* which specifically exempts 'property held for charitable purposes only, whether for a limited time or otherwise'.

Property ceasing to be held for charitable purposes

6.25 Problems can arise when settled property is held for charitable purposes only until the end of a period which may be defined either by date or by, for example, the happening of a particular event. The provisions are found in *IHTA 1984, s 70.*

IHTA 1984, s 70(2) provides that there shall be a charge under the section:

(a) where settled property ceases to be held for charitable purposes; and

(b) in situations other than (a) above where trustees make a disposition (again other than by application of property for charitable purposes) as a result of which the value of the settled property held for charitable purposes is less than it would be but or the disposition.

The section is an anti-avoidance section aimed at preventing individuals using a temporary charity to effect transfers free of IHT. There are, however, dangers for the bona fide charity which is careless in overstepping the bounds of its deed in the dispositions it makes. Particular care should be taken where the charity has the power to exercise a right of some kind (eg a right to acquire shares). If it deliberately decides not to exercise that right, it will be regarded as having made a disposition (*IHTA 1984, s 70(10)*).

As well as on the application of property for charitable purposes, an exemption to an *IHTA 1984, s 79* charge is also given in respect of the payment of costs or expenses in so far as they are attributable to property held for charitable purposes. Where the disposition is in the form of a payment which represents income, potentially assessable to income tax in the hands of the recipient, it will also be exempt from the *IHTA 1984, s 70* charge.

The rate of charge is highest for transfers made within ten years (0.25% for each of the first 40 complete successive quarters) and is reduced in successive ten-year bands.

Practical issues

The potential donor

6.26 As mentioned at **6.1** above, many charities push hard to persuade supporters to remember them in their wills. Some charities provide support in giving draft clauses to ensure that the legacy is correct and that there are no dangers of some of the issues of identification mentioned at **6.9** above applying. Some charities go further. Cancer Research UK, for example, offers a service called the FreeWill Service (FWS) which offers people aged over 55 the opportunity to make or update their wills with the charity bearing the cost. There is no obligation to make a gift to Cancer Research.

There are basically two types of wording that might be helpful to potential donors. The first applies where a donor wants to make a legacy of a proportion of his or her residuary estate, ie the balance of the estate after specific bequests have been made. The wording would be on the lines of:

> I give x% of the residue of my real and personal estate which I can dispose of by will in any manner I think fit to Charity Y (charity address and registration number) and the receipt of the Honorary Treasurer or the proper officer for the time being of Charity Y shall be a complete discharge to my executors.

The second will apply where a specific legacy is going to be given:

> I give the sum of £Z to Charity Y (charity address and registration number) and the receipt of the Honorary Treasurer or the proper officer for the time being of Charity Y shall be a complete discharge to my executors.

It is also suggested that the following wording should be added in any situation:

> If at my death the charity named as beneficiary in this will or any codicil hereto has changed its name or amalgamated with or transferred its assets to another body then my executors shall give effect to any gift made to such charity as if it had been made (in the first case) to the body in its changed name or (in the second case) to the body which results from such amalgamation or to which such transfer has been made.

Where the individual wants to leave some flexibility in making charitable legacies, then a bequest to something like the CAF might be appropriate. The task of deciding what to do with the money once it has reached the CAF account will then fall on the executors. The testator can consider providing a letter setting out his or her wishes which might be specific as far as particular charities or amounts are concerned, but might offer more general guidance, eg 25% to go to animal charities etc.

Executors

6.27 The role of the executors is to administer the estate. This will usually require a grant of probate in order for them to have the legal authority to dispose of the deceased's assets in accordance with his or her will. Probate cannot be granted until IHT has been paid and this will involve a calculation of the IHT payable, taking account of exemptions such as the charitable exemption. This can sometimes cause difficulties where there are legacies which are not exempt and some which are, and can be further complicated where some non-exempt legacies are stated to be free of tax. The particular issue comes in calculating the residue of the estate.

IHTA 1984, s 41 provides that the burden of tax is to be determined by ensuring that none of the tax on specific exempt gifts is to fall on those gifts and none of the tax attributable to property comprised in the residue is to fall on any exempt share of the residue.

The Inland Revenue takes the view that there is nothing to prevent the tax attributable to specific gifts made free of tax (FoT) being deducted from the whole residue before that residue is allocated. In calculating the tax relating to FoT legacies the formula used is:

$$\frac{\text{Grossed up value of specific gifts}}{\text{Total value comprised in chargeable estate}} \times \text{total tax on estate}$$

EXAMPLE 6.2

The net estate totalled £1,063,194.12 with total IHT payable of £81,078.09.

There were specific legacies free of IHT totalling £382,729.

There was a specific legacy of £90,000 to a charity.

The residue of the estate was divided as 3/4 to charity (in three equal shares) and 1/4 to a non-exempt beneficiary.

Stage 1 – calculate tax attributable to free of tax legacies

$$\frac{\text{Grossed up value of specific gifts (£507,070.23)}}{\text{Total value comprised in chargeable estate (£623,601.00)}} \times \text{total tax on estate (£81,078.09)} = \text{£65,927.22}$$

Balance of tax attributable to residue = £15,150.87

Stage 2 – calculate allocation of residue

Total estate		1,063,194.12
Less specific gifts free of tax	(382,729)	
specific exempt gift	(90,000)	(472,729.00)
Residue		590,465.12
Less tax attributable to FoT legacies		(65,927.22)
Balance of residue		524,537.90
Exempt part of residue (75%)		(393,403.42)
Balance of residue		131,134.48
Less balance of tax		(15,150.87)
Net balance of residue after tax		115,983.61

Summary of legacies

Specific legacies free of tax	382,729.00
Specific legacy to charity	90,000.00
Share of residue to charity	393,403.42
Balance of residue	115,983.61
Total legacies	982,116.03

Check back

Total estate before tax	1,063,194.12
Less tax	81,078.09
Estate net of tax	982,116.03

Chapter 7 Payroll Giving

Introduction

Background

7.1 The Payroll Giving Scheme was originally introduced in 1987 as a means of encouraging charitable giving by employees. Although the scheme was successfully used by some employers, the overall level of take up in the first ten years was disappointing and the Government used the Charities Tax Review to try to stimulate interest in the scheme.

The significant change introduced by the Charities Tax Review was the removal of the limit for donations under the scheme. When the scheme was first introduced the level of donations was set at £100 pa and this after great debate on the merits of £104 pa, £106 pa and £120 pa. The figure had been progressively increased and stood at £1,200 pa before the abolition of the limit. The logic behind the abolition is to encourage high earners to make the donations – although one could be cynical and suggest that if earners were not prepared to pay over £1,200, it seems unlikely that they will be prepared to make even larger donations.

To provide an added stimulus, in 2000 the Government introduced a 10% bonus which was added by the State to all donations under the Payroll Giving Scheme. This bonus came to an end on 5 April 2004.

Mechanics of the scheme in outline

7.2 Only those in employment can benefit from the scheme and only then if their employer is prepared to co-operate. The scheme operates by the employee authorising his employer to deduct his gift from his pay and pay it over to what is known as an agency charity which has been approved by the Inland Revenue. The agency charity acts as a clearing house distributing payments to charities nominated by the employee. The employee obtains his tax relief by having the amount of his donation deducted from his pay before any tax calculations are made under the PAYE scheme.

Key role of employers

7.3 The co-operation of the employer is clearly vital to the success of the scheme. There is no obligation on an employer to allow his employees to participate. They will have an additional administrative burden imposed on them but the early signs are that many employers have been prepared to co-operate. Some have gone as far as to set up agency charities to handle donations from their own employees. The employer is entitled to full tax relief against profits for the costs of establishing and running a Payroll Giving Scheme.

The fact remains that unless the employer is prepared to co-operate, the scheme cannot work, however much the employees may want it and however much charities may seek to promote it. There have been some remarkable success stories for large employers and some of these are mentioned at **7.17** below, but many employees work for small employers and it is persuading these small employers to absorb another area of administration that is one of the weaknesses of the scheme. The problem is more perception than reality, but the perception has to be overcome. A few years ago, the author participated in a series of seminars around the country aimed at promoting payroll giving. The seminars were aimed primarily at employers but charities were also invited. At each seminar, the number of employers present made up no more than 5% of the total audience. Perhaps instead of giving a 10% bonus to the giving, the Government should have given a cash incentive to every employer to establish a scheme, the overall results might have been greater.

Setting up a scheme

Introduction

7.4 There is a set-up process that must be followed for payroll giving, but once that process has been completed, the scheme should run smoothly and without too much hassle for the employer. The employer, of course, may be quite willing to take the initiative to establish the scheme and promote it to employees. This is probably much easier for a large company and it is no surprise that the examples of success which the Inland Revenue publicises on its website, and which are detailed at **7.17** below, are generally household names who are large employers. The smallest employer mentioned is one with 300 employees.

Sometimes the pressure for a scheme will come from employees, and responsible employers should respond to such requests in a positive way. Charities themselves are keen to promote the benefits of payroll giving and may approach employers directly, or may use one of the specialist payroll giving promotion firms to do the work for them.

Once the decision has been taken to set up the scheme, there are a number of clear stages to go through to get the scheme up and running. These are:

● establishing contact with an agency charity;

● promoting the scheme among employees;

● getting employees signed up;

● operating the deduction.

Role of the agency charity

7.5   The agency charity is pivotal to the scheme. It is this organisation that receives the payroll deductions from the employer and then distributes them to the charities chosen by the individual employees. The use of the agency charity is intended to ease the burden on the employer and it is possible for such a charity to act on behalf of a number of employers. They operate a standard agency agreement with each employer and this agreement must have Inland Revenue approval.

A further reason for the use of agency charities is that they make the job of the Inland Revenue in monitoring the system rather easier. Each agency wishing to be involved in the scheme must itself be a charity and must obtain approval from the Inland Revenue under the *Charitable Deductions (Approved Scheme) Regulations 1986 (SI 1986/2211)*. The Regulations provide that approval may be withdrawn or withheld if the Inland Revenue considers that the agency does not comply with the conditions it lays down. Those conditions include requirements that the agency must:

- have a contract with each employer;
- provide written receipts to the employer if requested to do so;
- not, under any circumstances, return to the employer or employees any amounts paid over to it;
- pay over to the nominated charities the amounts requested by the employees subject to any deduction for charges;
- provide, if requested by the employee, a certificate of the amounts paid over to charities nominated;
- not, under any circumstances, retain money. If it proves impossible to pay over to the nominated charity it must make payment to another with similar objectives;
- notify the Inland Revenue within 30 days of entering into an agreement with an employer;
- notify the termination of an agreement within 30 days;
- make an end-of-year return to the Inland Revenue;
- retain records for three years and make available those records for Inland Revenue inspection as required.

The Charities Tax Review has also led to legislation which requires the agency charity to pay over the funds to the end beneficiary charity within 60 days of the later of receiving the cash from the employer and receiving instructions from the employee as to allocation.

The charges which will be made by the agency charities will vary but a figure of 5% of amounts paid over will probably become typical. Employers will obviously check this at the start.

The agency charities which are currently on the Inland Revenue website are as follows.

Charities Aid Foundation
Kings Hill
West Malling
Kent ME19 4TA
www.giveasyouearn.org
0845 600 0366

Charities Trust
Suite 22, Century Building
Brunswick Business Park
Tower Street
Liverpool L3 4BJ
www.charities-trust.org
0151 284 2822

The Charity Service Ltd
6 Great Jackson Street
Manchester M15 4AX
www.payshare.org.uk

The Embassy of Man Payroll Giving Agency
725 The Whitehouse
9 Belvedere Road
London SE1 8YU
www.embassyofman.org.uk
0870 744 8789

KKL Payroll Giving Agency
58–70 Edgware Way
Edgware
Middlesex HA8 8GQ
www.kkl.org.uk
020 8421 7602
Sunninghill

Northern Ireland Council for Voluntary Action
61 Duncairn Gardens
Belfast BT15 2GB
www.nicva.org
02890 877777

Scottish Council for Voluntary Organisations
18–19 Claremont Crescent
Edinburgh EH7 4QD
www.scvo.org.uk
0131 556 3882

South West Charitable Giving
Churchtown
Peter Tavy
Tavistock
Devon, PL19 9NP
www.swcg.co.uk
01822 810094

Sovereign Giving
32 Highfields Mead
East Hanningfield
Chelmsford CM3 8AX
0161 839 3291

United Way Payroll Giving Service
PO Box 14
8 Nelson Road
Edge Hill
Liverpool L69 7AA
www.unitedtrusts.org
0151 709 8252

BEN – Motor and Allied Trades Benevolent Fund
(motor, motorcycle, bicycle and agricultural machinery sectors)
Lynwood
Rise Road
Ascot SL5 0AJ
www.ben.org.uk
01344 620191

Achisomoch Aid Company
(operates a charity voucher service)
35 Templars Avenue
London NW11 0NU
www.achisomoch.org
020 8731 8988

Promoting the scheme

7.6   The employer will need to spend time promoting the scheme among employees. There is plenty of help and advice available on this. All agree on one important starting point – there has to be support and enthusiasm for the scheme at the very top of the organisation. This can be supported by the employer agreeing some level of matching in donations, so that every pound which employees contribute through the scheme is matched by an agreed contribution from the employer.

It is important to establish how payroll giving is going to fit in with any other charitable activity within the employer. For example, will it be the only activity and simply be a way of allowing employees to give with no real employer involvement other than as facilitator, or will it be a key component of a corporate business strategy to give, which might already include a 'charity of the year' or some other type of charitable sponsorship?

Some employers may wish to do all the promotion work internally, on the basis that this will boost commitment. A group of employees could operate as a development team and could make use of publicity and support that is available. The Inland Revenue has produced information that can be used and this can be accessed on its website. The following is available:

- Toolkit Leaflet – A guide for charities explaining the Payroll Giving scheme, how to promote it and the resources available (PDF = Portable Document Format).

- ICFM Presentation in Powerpoint – A Powerpoint presentation by the Institute of Charity Fundraising Managers.

- Further Information:

    – a selection of documents in Word format offering advice and information about payroll giving;

    – looking after your donors;

    – promotion tips;

    – Professional Fundraising Organisations (PFOs) explained.

- Campaign Images – Images to download for use in your Payroll Giving campaign:

    – Employee's Guide;

    – A PDF (Portable Document Format) advertising the scheme to employees.

- Employer's Guide – A PDF advertising the scheme to employers.

- Poster – A poster advertising the Payroll Giving Scheme.

- Case studies – Four case studies are available in Word document format.

- Logos and Guidelines – Four versions of the Payroll Giving logo are available for downloading.

To obtain a hard copy of the Charities Toolkit (Leaflet and CD-ROM) call 08453 020203 or Minicom 0845 607 1234. (Lines are open 8am–8pm, Monday–Friday. Calls are charged at local rate.)

7.7   Payroll Giving

SPECIALIST PAYROLL GIVING ORGANISATIONS

7.7   Employers who do not want to use internal resources, can engage the services of a Professional Fundraising Organisation (PFO). There are a number of these organisations which specialise in promoting payroll giving. They may do so on behalf of specific charities or a group of charities, and may receive a fee from those organisations. They cannot exclusively promote those charities in payroll giving because employees must be free to direct their giving wherever they want. Care needs to be taken in choosing a reputable PFO and finding out how they are going to operate. The Inland Revenue publishes a list of PFOs on its website. These are all members of the Association of Professional Fundraising Organisations (APGPFO). The Inland Revenue list is accessible on its website and gives more details of each organisation. The basic details are as follows.

Giving@Work
White Stone House
Grange Paddock
Mark
Somerset TA9 4RW
www.givingatwork.co.uk
01278 641088

Charity Link
Grappenhall House
Hogmoor Lane
Hurst
Reading RG10 0DH
0118 934 4223

Charities Network
Springhill
Kennylands Road
Sonning Common
Reading RG4 9JT
www.charitiesnetwork.org.uk
0118 972 1421

Ease2Give
(Inland Revenue website states
APGPFO membership pending)
The Kilns
Kiln Road
Johnston
Haverfordwest
Pembs SA62 5ST
www.ease2give.com
01437 891911

Direct Donations (UK)
Prescot House
3 High Street
Prescot
Merseyside L34 3LD
www.directdonations2000.co.uk
0151 426 0144

Payroll Giving in Action
1st Floor
11A Litchdon Street
Barnstaple
North Devon EX32 8ND
www.payrollgiving.com
01271 342414

Prolific Donations Ltd
4 Davenant Road
Summertown,
Oxford OX2 8BX

Ringwood Oak
Ringwood Oak House
Minster Lovell
Oxfordshire OX29 0ND
01993 878877

Hands on Helping Charity
Fairfields
117 Castleton Road
Hope
Derbyshire S33 6SB
www.hands-on-helping.co.uk
01433 621882

Happy 2 Give
Beech Garth
Donnington Park
Newbury
Berks RG14 2DZ
01635 230346

Sharing the Caring
1st Floor West
Clarkson House
Rhodaus Town
Canterbury CT1 2RD
www.sharingthecaring.org.uk
01227 866866

Southern Payroll Giving Services
(Affiliated to IoF but not APGPFO)
1 Richmond Drive
Hayling Island
Hants PO11 0EP
023 9246 1440

Signing up employees

7.8 Employees who wish to participate in the scheme will need to sign a form authorising the employer to deduct a specified sum from their pay and to pay this over to the agency charity. There is no standard official form and employers can design their own to fit in with their scheme.

It will be seen as good practice to make sure that every deduction authorisation is properly acknowledged with a letter to the employee.

Operating the deduction

7.9 Once authorisation has been given, the employer can commence deductions from pay each week or month as appropriate. The deduction is effected from before-tax pay. The payroll giving deduction does not operate for National Insurance contribution (NIC) purposes, only for tax purposes. This means that both employers' and employees' NIC is calculated on the gross pay, but the employees' tax is on the pay net of payroll giving.

The employer must pay over to the agency the amounts deducted from pay within 30 days.

The employer has to keep records for at least three years and make them available to the Inland Revenue when requested to do so.

The employee's angle

What happens after the deduction?

7.10 Once the donation has been deducted from pay and paid over by the employer to the agency charity, the decision as to what to do with the funds is a matter for the employee. The set up process will include a mechanism by which employees can advise the agency of their decisions. Employees must have a totally free choice of charities to whom they can direct their donation. They cannot be bound by any links that the agency or any promoting fundraiser might have with specific charities.

The choice of charity and amounts can change. The only requirement is that the recipient must be a charity. The agency should be able to check if that condition is being fulfilled.

Obtaining tax relief

7.11 The employee obtains his or her tax relief immediately. The employee's tax bill each week or month is reduced because his or her taxable income is reduced by the gross amount of the donation. A monthly donation of £50 for a higher-rate taxpayer will mean a tax saving of £20 and, for a basic-rate taxpayer, a saving of £11. There is no further requirement to make a claim on a tax return or to deal with any other paperwork.

Payroll giving v Gift Aid

7.12 One of the keys to the future success of payroll giving will be if it is perceived as a more efficient way of giving to charity by high earners in particular. With the abolition of the limit on Gift Aid, any employee has to consider both routes as options for giving. There are three factors to consider:

- the impact of higher rate relief for the donor;
- when the donor gets the relief; and
- the tax recovery by the charity under Gift Aid.

If we take a simple example of a donation of £100, which can be made either as a cash donation under Gift Aid or as a deduction under payroll giving, we can make the following comparisons.

GIFT AID

7.13 Under Gift Aid, the donor pays £100 and the charity receives £128.20. A basic-rate taxpayer will obtain no further relief, but a higher-rate taxpayer will obtain further relief of £23 making the net cost of his or her donation £77. The higher-rate relief will usually come through the self-assessment return, although some relief for regular giving might be obtained through a coding adjustment if the taxpayer is in employment. This means that relief will be delayed until the tax payment date for the year, eg a donation in July 2004 will get tax relief on 31 January 2006 (although a claim could be made to backdate the relief to 31 January 2005).

PAYROLL GIVING

7.14 Under payroll giving, the donor has £100 deducted and the charity will receive £100. A basic-rate taxpayer will obtain tax relief of £22 making his or her net cost £78 and a higher-rate taxpayer will have tax relief of £40 giving a net cost of £60. Furthermore, the tax relief will be immediate in the calculation of tax for the pay period.

The ratio of net cost:amount received by the charity is the same in each case (1:1.66). Donors have to decide if the greater amount to the charity is more important than the instant tax relief that they will obtain.

The charity angle

Taking the initiative

7.15 Some charities have been very successful in plugging into payroll giving. They have taken the initiative either by direct promotion themselves or by engaging a PGO to work on their behalf. There may be opportunities for local charities to work with local employers to develop a new line of giving.

Ease of administration

7.16 Payroll giving is very easy on the charity administration and accounting system. The funds are received from the agency charities and nothing further is required. There is no tax reclaim process needed, and none of the detailed paper trail that Gift Aid requires.

Some success stories

7.17 The Inland Revenue website gives a number of success stories of payroll giving and four of these give a flavour of the components to a successful scheme that works for employers, employees and charities.

Brett Martin

7.18 Mallusk-based Brett Martin is a manufacturer of plastic drainage and sheet products, with 300 staff who seemed keen to support charities in different ways.

Brett Martin was not contracted to operate a scheme and its staff was unaware of the opportunity for tax-effective giving through the scheme. After meeting with a payroll giving promotion organisation, it asked them to help initiate a scheme, and to promote it to all its staff.

7.19 Payroll Giving

- **Brett Martin's Objectives:**
    - to offer its staff the opportunity to give through the scheme;
    - to fully inform its staff of how the scheme works;
    - to have a planned approach to promotion;
    - to actively promote the scheme throughout the company;
    - for employees to be able to give to any charity of their choice;
    - to generate positive local public relations.

- **Mechanics:**
    - the PFO advised Brett Martin's payroll department on the operation of the scheme;
    - the PFO arranged for a simple registration form to be forwarded to Brett Martin;
    - presentations were given to staff in their working environments including the shop floor;
    - the scheme was outlined to senior managers, who agreed a promotional schedule;
    - the PFO arranged for news releases announcing the outcome to local press.

- **Results:**
    - over two-thirds of the 300 staff joined the scheme after the initial one week promotion;
    - press coverage was gained in local and regional newspapers;
    - 232 staff joined, raising over £13,000 on an annual basis for a variety of different charities.

Inverclyde Council

7.19 This is a small council with 4,000 to 5,000 employees in Renfrewshire.

- **Inverclyde Council's objectives:**

    When approached by a professional fundraising organisation (PFO), the council was concerned about potential disruption to work. However, following discussion with the Head of Human Resources and with some departmental heads it was agreed that the PFO would do a pilot with the school cleaning services to gauge the effect before becoming involved with any other department of the council.

- **Mechanics:**

    Over a two-month period the PFO visited personnel on site at the schools and at the administration department, speaking to about 150 people.

● **Results to date:**

This achieved an 80% take-up, resulting in an annualised donation rate of about £6,000. As a result, the PFO is now discussing promotions with other departments within Inverclyde Council.

● **Charities:**

Inverclyde Council has contributed to a number of charities through its Payroll Giving scheme, including Childline (Scotland).

J Sainsbury

7.20 Sainsbury's original policy on the promotion of payroll giving was to allow local managers to make their own decisions. Over a period of time, stores experienced a number of unco-ordinated approaches from PFOs which led to some confusion amongst managers and staff, and caused extra administration for the company. In 1996, Sainsbury invited all PFOs to bid for preferred agency status and it selected an exclusive promoter.

● **Sainsbury's objectives:**

    –   to have one PFO work throughout the company;

    –   to offer the Payroll Giving scheme with a clear strategic plan;

    –   to increase its charitable commitment through staff involvement;

    –   to select a PFO with an ethos that would inspire confidence among its staff;

    –   to ensure that staff were able to give to any charity of their choice.

● **Mechanics:**

    –   the PFO submitted a work plan and timetable that detailed visits to all 370 locations over a one-year period;

    –   the PFO worked with Sainsbury to produce a donor pledge form acceptable to the company;

    –   the PFO contacted all sites and arranged promotions to suit local needs;

    –   follow-up visits were organised on a yearly basis.

● **Results:**

    –   over the past three years, 6,000 Sainsbury's staff have donated over £1m to a range of national and local charities;

    –   there is now an exceptionally low cancellation rate amongst Sainsbury's employees;

    –   Sainsbury was so pleased with the results after three years that it launched a new campaign called 'Thanks a Million';

–   'Thanks a Million' gets over the problem of contacting a largely shop-based staff by approaching them in canteens, where staff have a chance to speak to payroll giving promoters and get more information;

–   Sainsbury has commissioned a whole range of dedicated promotional materials for the campaign, including 'Thanks a Million' badges, using the PFO's design service;

–   twice as many Sainsbury's employees are joining this year as in previous years.

Yorkshire Water/Loop

7.21 Yorkshire Water has a long history of promoting involvement in the community, whether through providing volunteers or funding for locally-based campaigns, or being an active participant in the industry-led charity, Water-Aid.

After a successful Children's Promise campaign in 2000, Yorkshire Water and its sister company, Loop (customer management services), decided they wanted to develop their employee giving. With nearly 3,000 employees based in Yorkshire, Scotland and Wales, Yorkshire Water and Loop decided that the best way a successful campaign could be operated would be through using the services of a PFO.

● **Objectives:**

–   to make payroll giving a positive aspect of the employee benefit package;

–   to demonstrate the commitment of the business to community involvement, especially within our area of operations;

–   to allow all colleagues the opportunity to give through the scheme to any UK registered charity;

–   to make all colleagues aware of the added benefit to their chosen charity by giving through payroll giving rather than post-tax donations;

–   to run a planned, professional approach to the promotion.

● **Mechanics:**

–   the company chose a payroll agent and PFO to help them introduce and promote payroll giving. The PFO planned a structured awareness raising campaign of internal publicity that suited the cultures of Yorkshire Water and Loop, and advised and assisted in the production of promotional tools and branded literature for the launch;

–   co-ordinators of the company's Community Catalyst Fund agreed to provide funding and assistance in publicising the campaign across the various work locations;

- an internal website was set up with details of the PFO contacts, questions and answers, forms and further information about payroll giving;

- publicity and endorsement from the Executive Management Team was published in the company magazine;

- the PFO visited the major sites during a week-long launch of the Payroll Giving Scheme speaking to staff in differing working environments within Yorkshire Water and Loop.

● **Results to date:**

- within the first week staff joining the scheme pledged over £20,000 on an annual basis;

- the charities supported were wide-ranging including the Yorkshire Charities Group, Water Aid and the National Heart Research Fund.

- 138 employees are now giving over £36,000 per annum to 215 charities.

Summary

7.22 Since the introduction of payroll giving, over £70,000 will have been donated by the second anniversary.

Chapter 8   Raising Funds from Business

Introduction

A taxing problem

8.1   Charities have become very aware in recent years of the opportunities for generating funds from the business sector. A business wishing to make payments to charity will probably have a greater inclination to do so if it can obtain some relief against its own tax liability. Gift Aid provides some measure of relief, but is only given after the profits of the business have been calculated. A person running his or her own business can, of course, make payments out of his or her profits under Gift Aid. A company can also take the same route but will obtain no relief if it does not have profits liable to corporation tax against which it can set its qualifying donation. Ideally, businesses would like to have donations to charity allowed as an expense in arriving at profits, but the pathway to such a deduction is blocked by two major obstacles – *sections 74 and 577* of the *Income and Corporation Taxes Act 1988 (ICTA 1988)*. Although there has been some easing of the restrictions over the last few years, the problems remain substantial.

A basic trading deduction

8.2   *ICTA 1988, s 74* is the section which governs deductions which are allowable in computing the profits arising in a trade, profession or vocation, whether that trade is being carried on by a company, partnership or sole trader. The basic rule contained in *s 74(a)* is that the expenditure must be incurred 'wholly and exclusively for the purposes of the trade, profession or vocation'. This means that the trader has to show that the sole purpose for incurring the expense is for the purposes of his or her trade. If there is a dual purpose involved in the payment, then if one of those purposes is not for the business, that will disqualify the payment for tax relief. It will be very difficult indeed for a trader to claim that a straight gift to a charity is within *ICTA 1988, s 74(a)* even if he can show that some benefit in the form of increased sales may result from his benevolence. The link will usually be too indirect to meet the requirements of the section.

In giving judgment in the case of *Bentleys, Stokes and Lowless v Beeson (1952) 33 TC 491*, MR Justice Romer made the following comments on the meaning of 'wholly and exclusively' which clearly set out the difficulties that traders face in obtaining a deduction:

> It is conceded that the first adverb – 'wholly' – is in reference to the quantum of the money expended and has no relevance to the present case. The sole question is whether the expenditure in question was 'exclusively' laid out for business purposes, that is: What was the motive or object in the mind of the

two individuals responsible for the activities in question? It is well established that the question is one of fact: and again, therefore, the problem seems simple enough. The difficulty however arises, as we think, from the nature of the activity in question. Entertaining involves inevitably the characteristic of hospitality. Giving to charity or subscribing to a staff pension fund involves inevitably the object of benefaction. An undertaking to guarantee to a limited amount a national exhibition involves inevitably supporting that exhibition and the purposes for which it has been organised. But the question in all such cases is: Was the entertaining, the charitable subscription, the guarantee, undertaken solely for the purposes of business, that is, solely with the object of promoting the business or its profit earning capacity?

It is, as we have said, a question of fact. And it is quite clear that the purpose must be the sole purpose. The paragraph says so in clear terms. If the activity be undertaken with the object both of promoting business and also with some other purpose, for example, with the object of indulging an independent wish of entertaining a friend or stranger or of supporting a charitable or benevolent object, then the paragraph is not satisfied though in the mind of the actor the business motive may predominate. For the statute so prescribes. Per contra, if in truth the sole object is business promotion, the expenditure is not disqualified because the nature of the activity necessarily involves some other result, or the attainment or furtherance of some other objective, since the latter result or objective is necessarily inherent in the act.

ENTERTAINING EXPENSES

8.3   Expenditure on entertaining would, generally, fall to be considered as allowable under the basic deduction, however, the Inland Revenue became concerned that it was generally too easy to claim a deduction when there was a real benefit to the trader and so legislation was introduced to prohibit a deduction except in very limited circumstances. *ICTA 1988, s 577* provides that no deduction for Schedule D purposes is available for any expenses incurred in providing business entertainment. The section covers not only entertaining, such as hospitality, but also the provision of gifts unless the gift consists of an article incorporating a conspicuous advertisement for the donor. Even then the gift must not be food, drink, tobacco or a token or voucher exchangeable for goods and the cost of that article together with any others given to the same person must not exceed £10 (*ICTA 1988, s 577(8)*). There is some specific provision for gifts to charity and this is discussed below.

A partial solution

8.4   All is not doom and gloom for the business that would want to provide some tangible support for charity. There have been a number of provisions introduced in more recent years that provide some tax relief for gifts in kind. These have started off with very specific requirements but, in some situations, have become more generous. In addition, there may be some tax relief to be obtained in supporting charities through sponsorship, supporting research and also by making subscriptions. These will all be considered at **8.5** et seq and **8.15** et seq below. The final parts of the chapter will consider a new relief available for support of local community development (see **8.21** below) and also the possibility of establishing a corporate charitable trust.

Gifts in kind to charities

A general relief

8.5   The restrictions of *ICTA 1988, s 577* were highlighted at **8.3** above. The Inland Revenue is decidedly reluctant to allow a trader any relief for entertaining expenditure including gifts apart from the limited relief for small articles with conspicuous advertising such as pens or calendars or mouse mats. The provisions in *s 577(8)* would not give a great deal of hope to charities but, fortunately, some assistance is given by *s 577(9)* which specifically allows the making of a gift in kind to a charity. For the purposes of that subsection, the Historic Buildings and Monuments Commission for England and the Trustees of the National Heritage Memorial Fund are treated as charitable bodies.

It is still necessary for the trader to show that the gift has been made for the purposes of the trade, but this should not be difficult if some publicity or recognition is given for the gift. For example, a company may donate a significant prize for a charity raffle, or charity auction, and provided the programme for the event acknowledges the source of the gift that should be sufficient to justify the business deduction. Charities approaching traders for support in this way need to remember that they are not the only ones who will be making such requests, and, however good the cause, companies do not have a bottomless resource of gifts. Some companies set specific criteria as to who they will support – type of charity, location, type of event, profile of event, etc.

Gifts to local charities

8.6   There is also an Inland Revenue Extra-Statutory Concession B7 which gives some further scope. It reads as follows.

> *Section 577(8) ICTA 1988* provides that in general the cost of gifts is not an admissible deduction in computing profits chargeable under Schedule D or in management expenses claims. *Section 577(9)* removes this restriction in the case of business donations to registered charities (provided the deductions would otherwise be allowable) and a similar approach is taken to management expenses claims. Other expenditure on gifts is not regarded as within *section 577* provided that:
>
> (i)   it is allowable under *ICTA 1988, s 74(a) or ICTA 1988, s 75(1)*;
>
> (ii)   the gift is made for the benefit of a body or association of persons established for educational, cultural, religious, recreational or benevolent purposes, and the body or association is:

    (a)   local in relation to the donor's business activities; and

    (b)   not restricted to persons connected with the donor;

(iii) the expenditure is reasonably small in relation to the scale of the donor's business.

The payment of an ordinary annual subscription to a local trade association by a non-member is similarly not regarded as a gift provided condition (i) is met.

It is interesting to note that the type of association described in condition (ii) above is considerably wider than the generally accepted definition of a charity. In order to be within *ICTA 1988, s 74(a)*, the gift must probably have an 'advertising' element to it and the concession probably is intended to cover donations to bazaars and fundraising efforts being organised by local organisations who may not be charities.

Gifts of trading stock

8.7   This relief was originally introduced in 1991 as a means of encouraging businesses to donate equipment to educational establishments but was extended considerably by the *Finance Act 1999* to cover gifts made after 27 July 1999 to any charity or a body listed in *ICTA 1988,s 507(1)*, that is:

- Trustees of National Heritage Memorial Fund;

- Historic Buildings and Monuments Commission for England;

- Trustees of British Museum;

- Trustees of Natural History Museum.

The legislation, which is now *ICTA 1988, s 83A*, applies to gifts of articles which are manufactured by the trader or are of a class or description sold by the donor in the course of their trade. Where this happens, the value of the goods which are donated is ignored for tax purposes. This specific provision is required because it is a long-accepted principle of taxation that where a trader disposes of goods other than directly via a sale, a notional sale value has to be included. This crops up usually as 'goods taken for own use' and follows from a principle established many years ago by a case called *Sharkey v Wernher [1956] AC 58. Section 83A(3)* specifically states that:

    … no amount shall be required, in consequence of the donor's disposal of that article from trading stock, to be brought to account for the purposes of the Taxes Acts as a trading receipt of the donor.

The Inland Revenue has produced some guidance on how it interprets the legislation through what is referred to as a 'Revenue Interpretation' (RI). RI 151 deals specifically with donations of trading stock to charities and reads as follows:

    The Revenue have been asked about the tax treatment of trading stock donated to charities, for example, surplus sandwiches and other perishables which are given by retailers to charities for the homeless.

Except for trading stock given to 'designated educational establishments' (see below) there are no special rules governing the donations of trading stock, so normal Schedule D Case 1 principles apply. What are these principles?

Provided that the trading stock was originally manufactured and / or purchased in the ordinary course of trade, its later donation will not cause its cost to be disallowed for tax purposes. Neither does *ICTA 1988, s 577* (business entertaining expenditure and gifts) cause the cost to be disallowed.

Where the donation is made in the course of the trade, the amount to be credited in the trader's accounts will be the actual disposal proceeds, that is nil. The Revenue would accept that the donation is made in the course of the trade where the donation represents the most effective commercial way of disposing of the stock (for example where it would not be commercially effective to sell surplus perishable food).

Where a donation is not made in the course of the trade the amount to be credited in the trader's accounts for tax purposes will be the market value of the stock at the date of disposal. This follows the normal rule which applies where trading stock is disposed of otherwise than in the course of the trade. 'Market value' means the amount the stock could reasonably be expected to have realised in a market commercially available to the trader. It may be that there is no market for the stock commercially available to the trader, in which case the market value will be nil.

What this interpretation fails to really make clear is what is meant by 'in the course of the trade'. The donation needs to be seen as part of the ordinary process of the trader's business, eg fresh food not sold has to be disposed of as part of that process. Hopefully, the Inland Revenue will take a sympathetic view of circumstances where a trader makes a donation. Charities should keep an eye open for opportunities which might arise to utilise surplus stock.

There is one slight downside that needs to be watched out for – if, at any time, the donor or any person connected with them receives a benefit which is in any way attributable to the gift, he will be chargeable to tax on the value of the benefit. For example, if a charity gives tickets for a fundraising event to the trader as a thank you for the donation, there should be a tax charge on the trader.

Gifts of surplus equipment

8.8 Where a trader purchases plant and machinery for use in his or her business, he or she is not allowed to write off the cost of that equipment in the year of purchase, but can claim what are known as capital allowances for tax purposes. These allowances effectively give a controlled rate of depreciation over the life of the asset. The assets are put into a capital allowance pool when purchased and an allowance of 25% of the pool (after deducting the sale proceeds of plant disposed of) is given in calculating the taxable profits of the business. It is in the context of the disposal that there is a further tax break that can benefit charities. Where a trader disposes of plant and machinery that he or she has used in the business by giving it to a charity, a body within *ICTA 1988, s 507* (see **8.7** above) or a designated educational establishment (see **8.9** below), then in computing his or her capital allowances he or she is able to treat the disposal proceeds as nil (*Capital Allowances Act 2001, s 63*).

EXAMPLE 8.1

A local company has a van which has a trade-in value of £1,000. The company gives this van to a local charity. In calculating the value of the capital allowance pool, the company brings in a value of zero rather than £1,000, which means that the value of the pool stays unchanged and the company effectively continues to receive capital allowances on the van.

This particular relief applies not only to traders but also to persons carrying on a property letting business either in the UK or overseas and anyone running a furnished holiday lettings business.

Charities need to be on the look-out for firms who are renovating offices or upgrading equipment. Office furniture, computer equipment, other furniture, vehicles and, in some cases, more specialist equipment may all be available, and the charity needs to point out the advantages to the trader of making the donation.

Gifts to educational establishments

8.9   This relief pre-dated the wider relief in *ICTA 1988, s 83A* discussed at **8.7** above. The initial legislation relating to donations in kind made to 'educational establishments' remains in place in *ICTA 1988, s 84*, and is slightly more detailed than the general legislation in *s 83A*. The original section had reference to the gift of plant and machinery which is now in the *Capital Allowances Act 2001, s 63* and was discussed at **8.8** above.

The relief under *ICTA 1988, s 84(1)* now applies to:

   (a)   articles manufactured, or of a class or description sold, by the donor in the course of his trade which qualifies as machinery or plant in the hands of the educational establishment; . . .

The reference in *subsection (1)(a)* to the article qualifying as plant or machinery is amplified in *s 84(2)* which makes clear that the situation is a hypothetical one. If the establishment were treated as trading and if it had purchased the equipment then it would have qualified for capital allowances.

Again, the relief is given by excluding sale proceeds as under *ICTA 1988, s 83A*, but for this section to apply there must be a claim from the donor which specifies the equipment and the name of the educational establishment to which the donation was made. The claim must be made within two years of the end of the accounting period for a company, or by 31 January next but one after the end of the year of assessment for a trader within income tax.

The educational establishments which qualify are set out in the Regulations and are detailed in the *Taxes (Relief For Gifts)(Designated Educational Establishments) Regulations 1992 (SI 1992/42)* as follows:

PART I – SCHOOLS: ENGLAND AND WALES

1. Any school maintained by a local education authority.

2. Any grant-maintained school.

3. Any special school not maintained by a local education authority.

4. Any independent school registered pursuant to *section 70* of the *Education Act 1944* which is conducted by an educational charity.

5. Any school maintained by the Service Children's Education Authority.

6. The European School established under article 1 of the Statute of the European School, any school designated as a European School under article 1 of the Protocol to that Statute and the European School established under article 1 of the Supplementary Protocol to that Statute.

7. Any nursery school recognised by the Secretary of State for the purpose of receiving grant under *regulation 5* of the *Direct Grant Schools Regulations 1959 (SI 1959/1832)*.

PART II – SCHOOLS: SCOTLAND

1. Any public school.

2. Any self-governing school.

3. Any grant-aided school.

4. Any independent school managed by an educational charity.

PART III – ESTABLISHMENTS OF FURTHER AND HIGHER EDUCATION: ENGLAND AND WALES

1. Any university.

2. Any institution within the higher education sector (within the meaning of *section 91(5)* of the *Further and Higher Education Act 1992*) other than a university.

[3. Deleted]

4. Any institution of further or higher education (or both) maintained or assisted by a local education authority or in receipt of grant under regulations made under *section 100(1)(b)* of the *Education Act 1944*.

5. Any institution within the further education sector (within the meaning of *section 91(3)* of the *Further and Higher Education Act 1992*).

[6–22   Deleted]

23. Any other establishment providing further or higher education (or both) which is conducted by an educational charity.

PART IV – ESTABLISHMENTS OF FURTHER AND HIGHER EDUCATION: SCOTLAND

1. Any university.

2. Any central institution, college of education or any institution established under *section 77* of the 1980 Act.

3. Any establishment for the provision of further education under the management of:

    (a)   an education authority; or

    (b)   a company by virtue of *section 65* of the 1989 Act.

4. Any other establishment for the provision of further or higher education (or both) managed by an educational charity.

Gifts of medical supplies and equipment

8.10 A more limited relief is available for companies that hold stocks of medical supplies or medical equipment and make a gift out of their stocks for what the *Finance Act 2002, s 55* describes as 'humanitarian purposes'. Again, the relief is in the form of there being no sum brought into account for the value of the supplies gifted and, in addition, any expenses incurred by the donor in respect of transport or distribution are specifically deductible.

The relief is aimed at pharmaceutical companies that take part in disease eradication programmes under the auspices of national public health authorities, or international aid organisations of the World Health Organisation. It also covers practical responses to disaster relief.

Secondment of employees

8.11 Businesses of all kinds can obtain tax relief where they arrange for employees to be seconded to a charity or to an educational establishment. Relief for this expenditure is given by *ICTA 1988, s 86* which provides that the employer can claim a deduction for all the relevant expenses as if the individual had remained in their employment directly. This gets around the restriction imposed by *ICTA 1988, s 74* because such expenditure would not normally be accepted as being wholly and exclusively for the purposes of the trade.

The secondment of employees to the charity must be expressed and intended to be of a temporary nature. All the expenses relating to that employment (national insurance, pension costs, benefits, etc) can be allowed. The section does not define what it means by temporary, however, the Inland Revenue's own instructions tell Inspectors to accept a period of up to three years without enquiry. The section does not prescribe a limit on the number of employees who may be seconded at any time.

The section applies on secondment of employees to a charity and also to various types of educational establishment. These are defined in the section on a regional basis as follows:

- England and Wales:
    - a local education authority;
    - an educational institution maintained by such an authority;
    - an independent school within the meaning of the *Education Act 1996*, whose registration under *s 465* of that Act is final;
    - an institution within the further education sector, or higher education sector, within the meaning of the *Further and Higher Education Act 1992*.

- Scotland:
    - an education authority;
    - an educational establishment managed by such an authority within the meaning of the *Education (Scotland) Act 1980* (The 1980 Act);
    - a public or grant-aided school within the meaning of the 1980 Act;
    - a self-governing school within the meaning of the *Self Governing Schools etc (Scotland) Act 1989*;
    - an independent school within the meaning of the 1980 Act;
    - a central institution within the meaning of the 1980 Act;
    - an institution within the higher education sector within the meaning of *s 56(2)* of the *Further and Higher Education (Scotland) Act 1992*;
    - a college of further education within the meaning of *s 36(1)* of that Act.

- Northern Ireland:
    - an educational or library board within the meaning of the *Education and Libraries (Northern Ireland) Order 1986 (NI 3)*;
    - a college of education or a controlled, maintained, grant maintained, integrated, controlled integrated, voluntary or independent school within the meaning of that Order;
    - an institution of further education within the meaning of the *Further Education (Northern Ireland) Order 1997 (SI 1997/1772) (NI 15)*.

The section is one which should encourage a charity to approach companies who have employees skilled in particularly relevant areas to make the services of those employees available to the charity for short periods. One can think of the many needs of third-world charities for engineers of all kinds, agricultural experts as well as administrators, computer staff, etc.

Sponsorship

8.12 Commercial sponsorship has become a significant area of fundraising by charities and it has some particular tax significance for the charity depending upon how it is actually organised. The charity side of things is dealt with in detail in *Tolley's Charity Trading*. The other side to the coin is whether the sponsor is going to obtain tax relief for the sponsorship he or she has provided.

Inland Revenue guidance in this area is relatively generous. It points out that public companies are unlikely to spend large amounts on sponsorship without any obvious advertising benefits to their business. The Inland Revenue will look more closely at sponsorship by smaller companies where there could be an element of personal benefit, eg if a company sponsors the managing director's son's motor racing activity. There is unlikely to be any challenge to sponsorship for local or, indeed, national charities, provided that there is a clear advertising element as far as the business is concerned.

Payments to research associations, universities etc

8.13 Relief is available under *ICTA 1988, s 82B* where any trader:

- pays any sum to a scientific research association that has as its object the undertaking of scientific research related to the class of trade in which the trader is engaged and is approved for these purposes by the Secretary of State; or

- pays any sum to be used for such scientific research to any such university, college research institute or other similar organisation as is approved by the Secretary of State.

For these purposes, 'scientific research' is defined as being activities in the fields of natural or applied science for the extension of knowledge.

Subscriptions

8.14 Where a business pays an annual subscription to an organisation it needs to satisfy the 'wholly and exclusively' test to obtain a tax deduction against profits. The Inland Revenue guidance indicates the following:

- subscriptions for general charitable purposes are almost always made wholly or partly for non-business purposes and should not be allowed as deductions (Gift Aid will be a better route for these payments);

- if the trader has a direct trade connection with a charity or its objects, the Inland Revenue will allow a 'relatively' small annual subscription;

- subscriptions to churches, chapels, etc are not normally allowable, although in exceptional circumstances they might be regarded as staff welfare expenditure and could be allowable.

If it can be shown that the annual subscription to a charity could be claimed as a benefit to employees, then a deduction should be given. The Inland Revenue would want to see that the charity was available to the employee or immediate dependants if the need arose and that this could be regarded as a benefit to the employer's business. The Inland Revenue would disallow the payment if it considered it was of such a magnitude that it could only be regarded as arising from 'munificence'. The type of situations here would be a subscription to a local hospital or to a trade benevolent charity that related directly to the employer's business.

If the charity makes a special appeal and the employer, a regular annual subscriber, responds, the special payment can be allowed provided that the amount is reasonable and is not used for a capital project.

Business charitable trusts

A conduit

8.15 The concept of a charitable trust created by a business organisation is nothing new. Early entrepreneurs in the nineteenth century, with a social conscience or a Christian background, established foundations and trusts to provide education and welfare support in the communities where their businesses were located. The names of Rowntree and Cadbury in the confectionary industry are two examples. The tradition has been carried on by many businesses since then.

The trusts or foundations are established as registered charities. The funding comes from the business, probably now in the form of Gift Aid payments, but in the past, would have been fed by regular payments under a deed of covenant. These payments may be profit related. In many cases, where the business is an incorporated body, the charitable foundation will have a shareholding in that company and there will also be a dividend flow. In some situations, employees may also be able to make donations, perhaps via Gift Aid and possibly via payroll giving. Employees may also be able to nominate potential beneficiaries for the charity.

The charitable foundation is a means of directing corporate giving. There are many requests made to large businesses to support charitable causes. Some are supported with a blaze of publicity that generates tax relief in the form of sponsorship and the type of payments that have been discussed earlier in this chapter. Many requests are supported in a very quiet way using the charitable trusts.

Establishing a foundation

8.16 If a business decides that it wants to establish a charitable trust then it must go through the same process as anyone else who wants to set up a charity. The process involves creating a legal document, determining the objects of the charity and then seeking registration with the Charity Commission in England and Wales and dealing with the Inland Revenue in Scotland. The process is set out in detail in *Tolley's Charities Manual* and the Charity Commission publishes a very clear guide on the process and is very helpful in guiding prospective charities through the registration process.

Having established the charity, there are a number of other important decisions to take such as summarised below.

CREATING A LIST OF THE AREAS OF CHARITY THAT THE TRUST WILL SUPPORT

8.17   Some trusts decide to support only charities in a specific local area, some opt for particular types of venture, some decide that they will support only specific projects rather than making general donations to other charities, some concentrate on capital projects. Whatever policy is adopted it is helpful to have that clearly stated so that charities know what might be available and potential donors in the workforce know what their donations are going to support.

ESTABLISHING AN APPLICATION PROCESS

8.18   Once the existence of the charity is known, it will become inundated with requests from charities of all shapes and sizes and in all locations. The trust needs to have a clear process for acknowledging and processing those applications and for deciding how the limited resources are to be stretched to meet the unlimited demands. Depending on the size of the trust, it may have its own employees and offices, in some cases the responsibility will fall as part of an existing employee's portfolio. It needs to have a clear decision-making structure which is known by all those who are involved.

ENCOURAGING EMPLOYEE PARTICIPATION

8.19   Whilst the major core funding of the trust will come from the business itself, perhaps in the form of shares or significant profit-related donations, it is important to encourage employee participation. A Payroll Giving Scheme can be introduced, although this cannot require employees to make donations in the direction of the charity, but it may provide a spur to that. Gift Aid donations can be encouraged too. If the company is quoted, there may be advantages in pointing out the gift of share relief, particularly at times where share options are being exercised.

Whatever route is adopted it must be backed up by encouraging employee participation in the grant-making process. A number of employees should be involved directly in the decision-making process, and all employees should be able to nominate charities to receive funds.

The author writes this section on the morning after a quiz night run for a local charity in the town where he lives. £350 was raised, but one of the officers in the charity approached his employer – a large company – and the company agreed that its charitable trust would match the charity's profit pound for pound. The employee feels good that he has been able to generate this support and the company gains the publicity of having its generosity publicised at the event.

The charity angle

8.20 Corporate charitable trusts represent a significant source of finance for charities whether in the form of one-off donations, or some regular funding for a project. Charities seeking funds should remember that those funds are not bottomless and they are not the only charities seeking them. Many applications are rejected for every one that is fulfilled. Charities should take a little time to target their applications rather than simply trying the 'scatter gun' approach. A few practical issues to consider are suggested as follows.

- Do some research to identify the corporate charitable trusts – information is available in directories and on the Internet. That information often contains background on the types of grant that the fund will make and the grant-making process.

- Target the charity's applications. If the particular criteria that are stated do not match what the charity wants it is probably not worth applying. Do not think that there might be a bit of spare funds and the charity is such a good case that they are bound to give it to the charity. There are likely to be no spare funds – the trust could give away its funds many times over. It is better to target the charity's applications to a small number of charitable trusts whose criteria for grants the charity fits.

- Go for funding for a project. Many charitable trusts like to be associated with a particular project rather than simply making donations into the general funds of another charity. Identify a specific project that needs funding and focus the charity's application on that.

- Present the charity's application properly. A simple letter probably will not suffice. Produce a short paper that gives all the information about what the charity is trying to do, what the project is about, what funding the charity needs and what funding it already has in place. Make the presentation look attractive. If a hundred applications are being reviewed, make sure that the charity's stands out. Spend some time using a DTP system if the charity has access to one. If it does not, then very effective looking presentations can be produced using Word or Powerpoint which most people have access to on their computers.

- Time the charity's application properly. Many charitable trusts have a grant-making cycle that is geared into their own funding regime and the timing of their meetings. Information about this is often in the published information about the trust. Take note of it and make sure that the charity's application is submitted in plenty of time for the important meetings. Producing a wonderful presentation that is submitted a week after the main grant-making meeting will be a fruitless exercise.

- Express appreciation. If the charity's application is successful, write to thank the trust.

- Keep the trust informed. If the charity is successful and the project proceeds with the funding, tell the trust how it has gone. They will want to know and it may help if the charity makes further applications in the future. If the funding has been significant, invite someone from the trust to come down and see the project at first hand. Show them that the charity appreciates their support.

Community Investment Tax Relief

Introduction

8.21 Community Investment Tax Relief is a new scheme introduced by the *Finance Act 2002* which aims to provide tax relief for funding of projects in local communities. The funding comes from individuals and companies that invest in organisations known as Community Development Finance Institutions (CDFIs) which, in turn, provide funding for not-for-profit and profit-seeking enterprises in local communities. The tax incentive comes to the original investors and is a deduction for tax purposes that is spread over five years.

The scheme is administered jointly by the Inland Revenue, who deals with the tax reliefs, and the Small Business Service (SBS) of the Department of Trade and Industry (DTI), who are responsible for the accreditation of the CDFIs and monitoring their involvement in the scheme.

The investment

8.22 Tax relief is available to both individuals and companies. The basic criteria for relief is set out in the *Finance Act 2002, Sch 16, para 1*, which requires three basic conditions to be satisfied:

- the body in which investment is made is an accredited CDFI;

- the investment is a qualifying investment; and

- the investor has no control of the CDFI.

Investments qualify if they meet the following conditions:

(a) the investment consists of a loan, securities or shares that meet the conditions set out in the legislation;

(b) the investor has a valid tax certificate from the CDFI; and

(c) there are no arrangements which protect the investor against risks involved in the investment.

LOANS

8.23 If an individual or company makes a loan to a CDFI, the terms of which meet the requirements of the legislation, then tax relief is available. There are three basic conditions set out in the *Finance Act 2002, Sch 16, para 9*:

- *Condition 1* – the CDFI must receive all of the loan in one sum on the investment date, or have a drawdown facility which allows the full amount of the loan to be made within 18 months of the investment date.

- *Condition 2* – requires that the loan must not carry any present or future rights that would allow it to be converted into or exchanged for any loan, shares, securities or other rights which are redeemable within five years of the investment date.

- *Condition 3* – relates to the repayment terms of the loan and operates by reference to the so-called 'five years'. Basically, the legislation says that if the loan is repayable too quickly it will not qualify. The table below shows the maximum amount of the loan that can be repaid within each period if the loan is to remain a qualifying loan.

Table 8.1: Maximum loan repayments

Timing of payment within five-year period	*Upper limit of permitted repayment*
Year 1	No repayments permitted
Year 2	No repayments permitted
Year 3	25% of amount advanced
Year 4	50% of amount advanced
Year 5	75% of amount advanced

A requirement to repay that arises out of any obligation of the loan agreement is disregarded if the obligation:

- is imposed only because of the commercial risk to which the investor is exposed under the loan agreement; and

- is no more likely to be breached than any obligation that might have been expected to be imposed in the absence of the CITR scheme.

An example would be if the lender imposes a condition that the loan becomes repayable in the event of any default by the CDFI and it can be shown that any lender outside the CITR scheme would have imposed the same requirement.

If a bank that specialises in investing in charitable or social enterprises obtains accreditation as a CDFI, it is possible for a deposit account held by an investor in that bank to qualify for CITR. Withdrawal of funds from the account would then be regarded as a repayment of the loan.

SECURITIES

8.24   The conditions for securities are in the *Finance Act 2002, Sch 16, para 10* and require first that the securities must be subscribed for wholly in cash and be fully paid by the investment date. The second condition is that they cannot be capable of repayment, directly or indirectly within the five-year period. Indirect repayment would be via conversion to a loan or shares which were repayable inside the five-year period.

SHARES

8.25   The conditions for shares broadly follow those for securities.

TAX RELIEF CERTIFICATE

8.26   A CDFI must issue a tax relief certificate within 30 days of receiving an investment from an individual or a company. Where the investment takes the form of a loan with drawdown facilities, the certificate must still be issued within 30 days of the date of the first drawdown and will show the total amount of the loan but will indicate in the appropriate check box that the loan has a drawdown facility. Subsequent drawdowns do not require further certificates.

The form of the certificate is prescribed by the Inland Revenue and can be accessed through the Inland Revenue website.

The CDFI is limited in the amount of tax relief that it can certify in any year. The limits are:

- £10 million for what is known as a 'retail' CDFI; and
- £20 million for a 'wholesale' CDFI.

PRE-ARRANGED PROTECTION AGAINST RISKS

8.27   Relief is not available if the investor has some measure of protection against the risks to which they might expect to be exposed in the investment. Excluded arrangements can include insurance, indemnities, guarantees and other arrangements which may or may not be legally enforceable. Arrangements which might be put in place by a prudent investor, such as a charge on property owned by the CDFI, would not be excluded.

CONTROL OF THE CDFI

8.28   Tax relief is not available if the investor is able to control the CDFI, directly or indirectly at any time in the five-year period. Control of a company is usually determined by holding the majority of the voting rights either directly or with others who are connected persons, eg spouses and children etc.

Tax relief

BASIC RELIEF

8.29 The basic relief is 5% of the amount invested for five years, giving a total of 25% maximum. Individuals have their relief in tax years of assessment and companies gain theirs by reference to accounting periods.

EXAMPLE 8.2

An individual invests £20,000 in a CDFI on 20 August 2004. The amount subscribed forms the basis for the tax relief which will be £1,000 (5% of £20,000) for the year in which the subscription is made (2004/05) and £1,000 for each of the years 2005/06 to 2008/09.

EXAMPLE 8.3

A company which has a normal accounting date of 30 September, makes an investment of £20,000 also on 20 August 2004. It will obtain its first £1,000 of tax relief in its AP to 30 September 2004 and further relief of £1,000 in each of the APs up to and including that for year to 30 September 2008.

INDIVIDUALS

8.30 Individuals claim the tax relief via the tax return. A separate claim has to be made for each year. Although the claim cannot strictly be made until after the end of the tax year in which the investment is made, the Inland Revenue is prepared to give provisional relief through PAYE coding or through a reduction in payments on account under the self assessment system.

The relief is given as a deduction from taxable income. Therefore, in **Example 8.2** above where relief is £1,000 each year, if the individual was a 40% taxpayer, the value of the relief in tax terms would be £400. In the event that there is insufficient income to utilise the relief, there is no provision for carry forward or back and the unused relief will therefore be lost.

COMPANIES

8.31 A company claims tax relief after the end of the accounting period to which it relates, and a separate claim has to be made for each AP. The claim is made on the CT 600 return. Again, any excess relief cannot be carried forward or back.

DETERMINING THE INVESTED AMOUNT

8.32 The tax relief for both individuals and companies is based on the 'invested amount'. This is determined by the *Finance Act 2002, Sch 16, para 21*. In the case of shares and securities, the figure is straightforward being the amount subscribed by the investor.

The matter is more complex in the case of a loan because any repayments of the loan made in the five-year period will reduce the tax relief available. If no repayments are made, then the amount of the loan will determine the invested amount. Where repayments are to be made, the tax relief is based on the average amount of the loan outstanding over an appropriate period. This is referred to in the legislation as the 'average capital balance' and is defined as the mean of the daily balances of capital outstanding in the period.

Table 8.2: Invested amount on loans

Tax year or accounting period for which relief is due	Relief is based on (ie 5% of)
Year or period in which investment was made Year or period in which first anniversary of investment date falls Year or period in which second, third and fourth anniversaries of investment date fall	Average Capital Balance for first year of the loan. Average Capital Balance for second year of the loan. The smaller of: ● average Capital Balance for year that commences on the anniversary of the investment date that falls in that tax year; or ● accounting period; and ● average Capital Balance for the period of six months that ends on the second anniversary of the loan.

EXAMPLE 8.4

A company makes a loan of £100,000 to a CDFI. £10,000 is repaid at the beginning of the third year, and at the beginning of each subsequent year until the loan is repaid.

Accounting period	Average capital balance	Relief available
Period in which investment was made	£100,000	£5,000
Period in which first anniversary of investment date falls	£100,000	£5,000
Period in which second anniversary of investment date falls	£90,000	£4,500
Period in which third anniversary of investment date falls	£80,000	£4,000
Period in which fourth anniversary of investment date falls	£70,000	£3,500

RESTRICTIONS OF RELIEF

8.33 Relief may not be automatically available for the full five-year period. Relief cannot be claimed in any year if before the anniversary date of the investment in a particular year:

- some, or all of a loan has been disposed of by the investor;
- the loan has been completely repaid;
- repayments have exceeded the permitted limits;
- shares or securities have been disposed of;
- value has been received that exceeds the permitted limits;
- the CDFI has lost its accreditation.

WITHDRAWAL OF RELIEF

8.34 Relief can be withdrawn from the investor in a number of circumstances, and may be reduced in others. The withdrawal is effected by an assessment to tax under Case VI Schedule D for the year of assessment or accounting period for the year in which relief was originally given. (*Finance Act 2002, Sch 16, para 27*). The three basic circumstances which may trigger withdrawal of some, or all, of the relief are:

- disposal of loan;
- disposal of shares;
- receipt of value.

All of these must take place within the five-year period. Cessation of ownership by reason of the death of the investor is not regarded as a disposal

Relief is to be reduced if the investment is disposed of:

- at arm's length to an unconnected party;
- by way of distribution in a winding up of the CDFI;
- by reason of the entire loss of the asset under the negligible value rules;
- after the CDFI has lost its accreditation.

The disposal proceeds, if any, reduce the tax relief available in respect of the original investment. If, in any year, the investor's income was not sufficient to utilise all the relief claimed, the amount of the reduction is 5% of the disposal proceeds.

EXAMPLE 8.5

An individual subscribes for £30,000 shares in a CDFI on 1 June 2004. On 1 January 2008, the investor sells a third of the shares for £10,000 in an arm's length deal. The investor has been able to utilise all the relief claimed.

8.35   Raising Funds from Business

Immediately before the sale the relief that would have been claimed would be £1,500 (5% × £30,000) for the years 2004/05, and 2005/06. The claim in respect of 2006/07 would fall to be made no later than 31 January 2008 when the return for that year had to be filed. The claim for that year may already have been made.

The disposal means that the claims made for 2004/05, 2005/06, and possibly 2006/07, each have to be reduced by £500 (5% × £10,000) and the claims to be made for 2007/08 and 2008/09 (and possibly 2006/07 if not already made) are to be in the sum of £1,000.

RECEIPT OF VALUE

8.35   The legislation specifies the situations in which value is deemed to have been received (*Finance Act 2002, Sch 16, para 35*). These situations can be summarised as follows in **Table 8.3**.

Table 8.3: Circumstances in which value is received

Circumstances in which value is received	Amount of value received
Repayment, redemption or repurchase of any securities or shares.	Amount received by the investor.
Release or waiver of any liability of the investor, or discharging or undertaking to discharge any liability of the investor to another person.	Amount received by the investor.
Making of a loan or advance to the investor that is not fully repaid before the investment is made.	Amount of the loan less any amount repaid before the investment is made.
Provision of a benefit or facility to the: ● Investor; ● associate of the investor; ● directors or employees of corporate investors, or any associates of those directors or employees.	Cost of providing the benefit or facility less any consideration given for it by the investor or any associate of the investor.
Disposal of an asset to the investor for less than market value.	The difference between the market value of the asset and any consideration given for it.

Table 8.3: Circumstances in which value is received – *contd*

Circumstances in which value is received	*Amount of value received*
Acquisition of an asset from the director at more than market value.	The difference between the market value of the asset and any consideration received for it.
Making of any payment to the investor.	The amount of the payment.

Where the investment is in shares or securities, the relief will be withdrawn if the value received during the year preceding the investment or the five years following exceed the limits shown in the table below. Where value received is within the permitted limits, the tax relief is reduced rather than being withdrawn.

Table 8.4: Timing of receipt of value

Timing of receipt of value within period of investment	*Permitted Level of Receipts*
Year preceding investment	No receipts are permitted
Years 1 and 2 of investment	No receipts are permitted
Year 3	Up to 25% of invested amount
Year 4	Up to 50% of invested amount
Year 5	Up to 75% of invested amount

EXCESSIVE LOAN REPAYMENTS

8.36 Provisions in the *Finance Act 2002, Sch 16, para 30* cause relief to be withdrawn if the original investment is by way of loan and what the legislation terms 'excessive' repayments are made. These are repayments that cause the average capital balance of the loan to fall below prescribed limits summarised in **Table 8.5** below.

Table 8.5: Excessive loan repayments

Year of Loan	*Average capital balance must not be less than*
Year 3	75% of the average capital balance for the period of six months beginning 18 months after the investment date
Year 4	50% of the average capital balance for the period of six months beginning 18 months after the investment date
Year 5	25% of the average capital balance for the period of six months beginning 18 months after the investment date

Accreditation of CDFIs

8.37   The responsibility for accrediting CDFIs rests with the Small Business Section of the DTI and information on the accreditation process can be found on their website at www.sbs.gov.uk. A list of the CDFIs accredited to date is set out below. Charities involved in ventures in the relevant areas should consider contact with these organisations to establish if funding for projects might be available.

Name and address of CDFI	Contact details for CDFI		Scope of operation of CDFI
Aspire Micro Loans for Business Ltd 5 Union Street Belfast BT1 2JF Northern Ireland	Niamh Goggin Tel: 028 9024 6245 Fax: 028 9024 6255	Email: mail@aspire-loans.com www.aspire-loans.com	Self-employed and micro-entrepreneurs in Northern Ireland
Aston Reinvestment Trust (ART) The Rectory 3 Tower Street Birmingham B19 3UY	Steve Walker Tel: 0121 359 2444 Fax: 0121 359 2333	Email: reinvest@gn.apc.org www.reinvest.co.uk/	Businesses in Birmingham and Solihull
BIGinvest Company Ltd 1–5 Wandsworth Road London SW8 2LN	Leonie Hirst		Wholesale lending to CDFIs across the UK
Black Business in Birmingham Unit 7, 3b Business Village Alexander Road Handsworth Birmingham B21 0PD	Goriola Sonola Tel: 0121 523 1820 Fax: 0121 554 8823	Email: owen@3b.org.uk www.3b.org.uk/	Ethnic minority entrepreneurs in Birmingham
Black Country Reinvestment Society (BCRS) Social Economy House Victoria Street West Bromwich B70 8ET	Paul Kalinauckas Tel: 0121 5532620	Email: enquiries@bcrs.info	Social enterprises in Dudley, Sandwell, Walsall and Wolverhampton
Bolton Business Ventures (BBV) Ltd Bolton Business Cente 46 Lower Bridgeman Street Bolton BL2 1DG	Paul Davidson Tel: 01204 391400	Email: prd@bbvonline.net	Businesses in Bolton, Bury, Oldham, Rochdale and Wigan
Charity Bank PO Box 295 25 Kings Hill Avenue West Malling Kent ME19 4WD	Malcolm Hayday Tel: 01732 520029 Fax: 01732 520123	Email: enquiries@charitybank.org www.charitybank.org/	Charities across the UK

Name and address of CDFI	Contact details for CDFI		Scope of operation of CDFI
Derby Loans Group Suite 17 Rosehill Business Centre Normanton Derby DE23 6RH	Andrew Baker Tel: 01332 365550 Fax: 01332 344411	Email: info@derbyloans.co.uk www.derbyloans.co.uk	Businesses in the city of Derby
The Enterprise Fund 90 Great Bridgewater Street, Manchester M1 5JW	Bob Marchant Tel: 0161 245 4977 Fax: 0161 237 9458	Email: info@enterprisefund.co.uk www.enterprisefund.co.uk	Businesses in the Greater Manchester Sub-region
First Enterprise Business Agency 82–84 Radford Road Forest Fields Nottingham NG7 5FU	Richard Tyas Tel: 0115 942 3772 Fax: 0115 9421504	Email: info@first-enterprise.co.uk www.first-enterprise.co.uk	Ethnic minority entrepreneurs in the East Midlands
Industrial Common Ownership Finance (ICOF) 227c City Road London EC1V 1JT	Andrew Hibbert Tel: 020 7251 6181 Fax: 020 7336 7407	Email: icof@icof.co.uk www.icof.co.uk/home.htm	Co-operatives and social enterprises across the UK
Local Investment Fund (LIF) 123 Minories London EC3N 1NT	Roger Brocklehurst Tel: 020 7680 1028 Fax: 020 7488 9231	Email: information@lif.org.uk www.lif.org.uk	Community and social enterprises across the UK
London Rebuilding Society (LRS) 227c City Road London EC1V 1JT	Naomi Kingsley		Social enterprises across London
One London 28 Park Street London SE1 9EQ	Peter Thackwray Tel: 020 7403 0300 Fax: 020 7248 8877	Email: info@one-london.com www.gle.co.uk/onelondon	Wholesale lending to CDFIs in London
National Federation of Enterprise Agencies (NFEA) Trinity Gardens 9/11 Bromham Road Bedford MK40 2UQ	George Derbyshire Tel: 01234 354055	Email: enquiries@nfea.com www.nfea.com	Finance for SME clients of member Enterprise Agencies nationwide
North Staffordshire Risk Capital Fund (NSRCF) Limited Bentley Jennison 5 Ridge House Festival Park Stoke-on-Trent ST1 5SJ	Chris Cummings Tel: 01782 262121		Businesses in Stoke-on-Trent, Staffordshire Moorlands, Newcastle-under-Lyme and Stafford

8.37   Raising Funds from Business

Name and address of CDFI	Contact details for CDFI		Scope of operation of CDFI
The Prime Initiative Astral House 1268 London Road London SW16 3ER	Nigel Foyster Tel: 020 8765 7851 Fax: 020 8765 7879	Email: prime@ace.org.uk www.primeinitiative.org.uk	Focusing on the over-50s starting new businesses across the UK
Social Investment Scotland Level 3 Orchard Brae House 30 Queensferry Road Edinburgh EH4 2UZ	David Herd Tel: 0131 315 8100	www.socialinvestment scotland.com	Wholesale lending to not-for-profit CDFIs across Scotland
Triodos Bank Brunel House, 11 The Promenade, Clifton, Bristol BS8 3NN	Matthew Robinson Sue Cooper Tel: 0117 980 9700	www.triodos.co.uk	On-lending to organisations with social and cultural value across the UK
Ulster Community Investment Trust 13–19 Linenhall Street Belfast BT2 8AA Northern Ireland	Trudi Dunlop Tel: 028 9031 5003 Fax: 028 9031 5008	Email: info@ucitltd.com www.ucitltd.com/ welcome.asp	Working through Community Economic Development Organisations in Northern Ireland
West Yorkshire Enterprise Agency New Commerce House 168 Westgate Wakefield WF2 9FR	Brian Hatcher Tel: 01484 438800	Email: brian.hatcher@blwy.co.uk	Entrepreneurs in West Yorkshire
Yorkshire Enterprise Group Saint Martin's House 210–212 Chapeltown Road Leeds LS7 4HZ	Peter Claydon		Lending to micro enterprises across Yorkshire

Chapter 9   Keeping the Regulators Happy

Introduction

9.1   Trustees of charities must always keep in mind that they do not operate in a
laissez faire situation because charities are subject to a regulatory regime in the
UK which, in the context of giving, will involve two government bodies – the
Charity Commission and the Inland Revenue. These two bodies will monitor
charities and will step in where they believe there are problems. Their roles, in
the context of giving, are different. The Charity Commission is primarily concerned to protect charitable funds and will act to deal with problems that affect
both charities and donors. The Inland Revenue is concerned with ensuring that
the tax benefits associated with giving in all the areas considered in this book
are not abused either by charities or donors.

This chapter will briefly explain the organisation of each regulator and the
method by which they operate. It will then consider the particular issues that
arise in relation to giving and consider how the regulators deal with these
issues. Charities who find themselves on the wrong end of such enquiries need
to take careful advice. More background on these issues and how to handle
them can be found in Burgess A, *Tolley's Charities Investigations* (2002)
(LexisNexis).

The Charity Commission

Development

9.2   The Charity Commission took its present form following the *Charities Act
1960*, although their origins go back to the mid-nineteenth century when the
Charitable Trusts Act was passed in 1853. This Act set up a Body of
Commissioners who were supported by a staff of inspectors with powers to
enquire into the state of a charity, to give reliable legal advice to trustees, to
sanction transactions in charity property and to control the bringing of charity
law suits.

Legal powers

9.3   The *Charities Act 1993, s 1(1)* states that:

> There shall continue to be a body of Charity Commissioners for England
> and Wales, and they shall have such functions as are conferred on them by
> this Act in addition to any other functions under any other enactment for the
> time being in force.

This reflects the fact that the Commissioners were originally created by the 1960 Act, and indicates the pivotal role that the Commissioners have in the regulatory framework for charities. The section goes on to give two general functions and objects for the Commissioners:

(3) The Commissioners shall (without prejudice to their specific powers and duties under other enactments) have the general function of promoting the effective use of charitable resources by encouraging the development of better methods of administration, by giving charity trustees information or advice on any matter affecting the charity and by investigating and checking abuses.

(4) It shall be the general object of the Commissioners to act in the case of any charity (unless it is a matter of altering its purposes) as best to promote and make effective the work of the charity in meeting the needs designated by its trusts; but the Commissioners shall not themselves have power to act in the administration of a charity.

The roles are essentially on two levels – to provide support to the charitable sector as a whole, but also, significantly, to get involved in the activities of individual charities. Charity trustees should recognise the benefits of using the Commissioners as a source of information and advice, but must also realise that their own actions may be subject to the closest possible scrutiny by the Commissioners.

Geographical organisation

9.4   The Commissioners have three offices located in London, Liverpool and Taunton. All three offices do the same type of work, but this is distributed between offices on a geographical basis. The location of a charity (usually found in the correspondent address) determines which office is responsible.

The current addresses of each office are as follows:

London
Harmsworth House
13–15 Bouverie Street
London EC4Y 8DP

Liverpool
20 Kings Parade
Queens Dock
Liverpool L3 4DQ

Taunton
Woodfield House
Tangier
Taunton
Somerset TA1 4BL

There is now a single telephone contact number for general queries covering all the offices, and this is 0870 333 0123. The number for hearing and speech impaired callers using a minicom is 0870 333 0125.

It should be noted that the Commission does not operate in Scotland. Issues of charitable status are resolved by the Inland Revenue in Edinburgh and powers which need to be exercised under the *Law Reform (Miscellaneous Provisions) (Scotland) Act 1990* are carried out by the Scottish Charities Office which is located at:

Crown House
25 Chambers Street
Edinburgh EH1 1LA
Tel 0131 226 2626

Functional organisation

9.5   The functional organisation within each office broadly breaks down into two main areas as far as charities are concerned – support and investigation. The former exists to provide help and advice to charities. Dealing with issues relating to helping charities to function better, producing schemes to enable charity assets to be used more effectively, or perhaps to enable charities to merge to create a more efficient unit. The latter group are heavily engaged in making charities accountable and reviewing the activities of those engaged in the charitable sector. It is their role that will be the focus of attention in **9.9** below.

The Commission has traditionally had a strong legal element in its staff. The production of schemes, the handling of property issues, trust law and so forth all requires a legal approach. In more recent years there has been a major move to recruit accountants and to develop the financial side of the Commission. This is particularly true of the investigation area where the examination of accounts and financial records assumes an important role.

Although the two main strands are separately organised, there is a great deal of co-operation between the two groups. The investigation group will often refer issues they uncover to the support side to resolve with the charity because that is the best solution for the charity concerned. The support side may well uncover issues which require a more investigative approach.

Legal Framework

9.6   The current main legislation governing charities is the *Charities Act 1993* which consolidated most of the powers set out in the *Charities Acts 1960* and *1992*. There are also a number of Regulations. At the time of writing there is a draft Charities Bill awaiting detailed consideration. The *Charities Act 1993* applies only to England and Wales. Some of the provisions are paralleled in Scotland by the *Law Reform (Miscellaneous Provisions) (Scotland) Act 1990* which came into effect in the autumn of 1992.

Inland Revenue

Introduction

9.7   The Commissioners of Inland Revenue (usually referred to as the 'Board') are given the care and management of income tax, corporation tax and capital gains tax by *s 1* of the *Taxes Management Act 1970 (TMA 1970)*. The Commissioners themselves hold office by virtue of the *Inland Revenue Regulation Act 1890*. The organisation over which the Board preside is a huge one – one of the largest of the government departments and one which has seen many changes of organisation over recent years as it has tried to come to grips with the demands of collecting tax in a very different economic, cultural and technical setting to that into which income tax was originally introduced in 1799.

The traditional Inland Revenue structure, as far as the taxpayer is concerned, has been based on the local district. That structure is changing and is being streamlined with many taxpayers finding that they no longer have a local tax office. The long established title of Inspector of Taxes is also being phased out to be replaced by 'officer of the Board', which the more traditional among us find less attractive!

As far as charities are concerned, the change in local district structure is not likely to have any major impact except in the area of employer compliance, because the Inland Revenue has long recognised that the tax affairs of charities needed special attention. There are, therefore, two faces of the Inland Revenue for charities:

- Inland Revenue (Charity) which deals with the tax affairs of the charity itself;

- PAYE district which handles the tax affairs of the charity's employees and deals with the compliance of the charity with the requirements of PAYE.

Inland Revenue (Charity)

9.8   The Inland Revenue recognised many years ago that it needed to have a special unit to deal with the tax affairs of charities. This was largely because the work was primarily that of dealing with claims for repayment of tax and because the tax regime relating to charities was so very different to that of other entities and individuals. The work in dealing with charities formed part of a division known as the Claims Branch (Charity Division). That division has gone through a number of changes of title and identity and currently sits as part of a large unit which deals not only with charities, but also handles issues relating to major financial intermediaries (such as the operation of the MIRAS scheme) as well as matters relating to advice on non-residence and the UK tax affairs of offshore trusts.

The main office is based in Bootle in a very impressive new Inland Revenue building. There is also an office in Edinburgh (Inland Revenue (Charity)

Scotland), which has an important role for all charities in Scotland because it is the office which determines whether those organisations can be regarded as charities in Scotland. The offices are staffed by Inland Revenue personnel who have come into the office from the main tax district network. They are not specialists in charity taxation, but they have to become so in a very short period of time because they are the Inland Revenue's specialists in this area.

The role of Inland Revenue (Charity) in respect of charities is to review the entitlement to tax exemption and to ensure that charities comply with the tax law as it affects them. The Inland Revenue no longer has to establish the charitable status of organisations. As far as registered charities are concerned, that is now the role of the Charity Commission, although that department does contact the Inland Revenue as part of the registration process. In the days before the Charity Commission came into being, the Inland Revenue was the arbiter of charitable status because tax exemption was the prime benefit of that status. Inland Revenue (Charity) will still need to consider whether an organisation which is not required to register with the Charity Commission, is in fact an organisation which has been established for charitable purposes only. It will have to take its own decision on this.

The basic work of the unit in Inland Revenue (Charity) can be identified as follows.

- Processing tax repayment claims made by charities – these are primarily in the area of Gift Aid. The approach adopted in the repayment process is largely a 'repay now, check later' one although some more detailed checks are undertaken on the first claim made and on a sample of other repayments.

- Charity audit visits to check on claims for repayment of tax on qualifying donations under the Gift Aid regime and formerly under deed of covenant donations. This usually involves a field visit to the charity.

- Issue of self assessment returns to charities and the review of those returns – this is a modification of the old system of examining the accounts of charities that were submitted on a voluntary basis. The system of self assessment establishes the investigation framework. In broad terms, it will involve checking the entitlement to tax exemption on matters such as trading and fundraising activities. It also involves examining the accounts of companies which are wholly owned by charities.

- Providing advice to charities on a range of technical issues, such as the possible tax treatment of certain receipts, whether activities amount to trading which might or might not be exempt etc. Charities who have interesting tax issues will find benefit in discussing them with the Technical and Advisory people in Inland Revenue (Charity) before they implement them. Major problems can be easily averted.

Charity Commission investigations

Introduction

9.9   The Charity Commission identifies one of its main objectives as being 'to identify and deal with abuse and poor practices'.

This has become a more significant area of the work of the Commission, and more specialist resource has been directed towards it. The development of the work has also been assisted by the development of a framework of legal accountability for charities put in place by the *Charities Act 1993*. In particular, the requirements to make annual returns provides a ready source of review material.

Legal framework

9.10   The power of the Charity Commission to carry out enquiries stems from the *Charities Act 1993, s 8(1)*, which states that:

... the Commission may from time to time institute inquiries with regard to charities or a particular charity or class of charities, either generally or for particular purposes, but no such inquiry shall extend to any exempt charity.

The power is deliberately drawn as widely as possible to give the Commissioners the ability to act in a variety of situations. It should be noted that the power extends to investigations into excepted charities but not exempt charities.

The remainder of *s 8* deals with the process of investigation. Other provisions relating to investigations include:

- *section 9* – power to call for documents and search records;

- *section 10* – disclosure of information to and by the Commissioners;

- *section 11* – supply of false information to the Commissioners.

Investigation issues

9.11   Investigations can cover a wide range of areas, but issues relating to fundraising, which will cover giving are one of the major areas of interest. Reports on concluded investigations are now published on the Charity Commission website and provide interesting, but chastening, reading. Examples of these reports are mentioned at **9.20***ff.*

INVESTIGATION PROCESS

9.12   The process of investigation work falls into a number of clear stages:

(a)   initial information indicating a potential problem – this can come from a variety of sources including members of the public, charity supporters, or from a review of the annual return;

(b)   evaluation of the evidence and an initial review to see if the case needs a full investigation – in many cases this process either establishes that the concerns are not founded or enables the specific areas of concern to be cleared;

(c)   investigation under the power in the *Charities Act 1993, s 8*;

(d)   remedial action as necessary using the powers in the *Charities Act 1993*.

INVESTIGATION ORGANISATION

9.13   Each of the three offices of the Commission has an investigation team, which comprises administrative staff who have some background knowledge of the charity sector and have investigative skills. They are able to call upon the legal and accountancy teams in each office for support where needed. They do have training on investigative techniques and questioning and a detailed Enquiry Manual is currently being produced, extracts from which should eventually appear within the public domain in the Operational Guidance Notes available on the Charity Commission website.

CHARITY COMMISSION PUBLICATION CC47

9.14   The Commissioners produce a range of publications and one publication is available on 'Inquiries into Charities' (CC47). This explains in outline terms:

● the types of complaints they consider;

● how members of the public can alert them;

● confidentiality;

● what happens when they are alerted;

● formal enquiries;

● action to put things right;

● auditor and examiners duties.

Fundraising abuse

INTRODUCTION

9.15   This has been a growing area of investigation. Common problems are:

● the offer of funds from professional fundraisers who have not been appointed by the charity;

● aggressive fundraising techniques being employed either by the charity or by fundraisers acting on their behalf;

● too much money going to the fundraisers and not to the charity;

● the use of bogus charities to collect money.

This latter example highlights a significant legal issue relating to the jurisdiction of the Charity Commission to act in cases where those involved in the problem are not charities themselves. Back in their 1998 Report, the Commissioners gave two actual examples of fundraising cases they had investigated. In one case, involving the selling of roses through pubs and clubs, criminal activity was uncovered and the matter was referred to the police who mounted a successful prosecution. In another case, the Commissioners investigated two organisations, neither of which were registered charities, where one was raising money on behalf of the other which described itself as a 'registered charitable institution'. The Commissioners made orders prohibiting further fundraising and effectively drove the companies out of existence.

These cases prompted the following comment from the Commissioners (at p 23 of the 1998 report):

> The individuals behind these operations sometimes believe that, as their organisations are not charities, we have no jurisdiction over them. However, it has been our view, which has been backed up in a court judgement, that we do have jurisdiction over the funds they hold, if they have been raised via a charitable appeal.

There are two cases in which the Commission have been successful in dealing with individuals who sought donations, and these cases have been upheld in another case which went to judicial review. What the cases show is that where a person acts as a fundraiser for a charity (whether he or she has been formally asked or appointed or not) he or she becomes, in reality, a trustee of the funds he/she collects. Those funds are funds held for charitable purposes and hence the Charity Commission have jurisdiction to act.

In the case of *Jones v Attorney General [1974] ch 148*, charity collectors using open boxes had taken a commission out of the boxes with the knowledge of the trustee/founder of the charity concerned who was appealing against the decision to remove him as a trustee. In the judgment, Mr Justice Brightman stated:

> 'a person who solicits money for a charity is a trustee of the money for the purpose of handing it to the charity. A member of the public who puts money in the box is the donor of his contribution, not indistinguishable, in principle, from any other donor or settlor of trust funds. Unless the collector makes known to the donor his intention to retain a percentage of the contribution for himself, it seems to me that he has no possible title to that percentage.

This judgment was followed in the case of *Rv v Wain [1995] 2 Cr App Rep 660* which concerned an individual who ran events to raise money for a Television Telethon. He put the money into a bank account, but then transferred sums to his own private account. Cheques were drawn to pay to the TV company but they were not honoured. Wain claimed that the money in the bank account did not belong to the TV Trust, but it was simply an unsecured creditor. He was convicted of theft but appealed. In turning down his appeal, Lord Justice McCowan remarked:

It seems to us that by virtue of *section 5(3)* [of the *Theft Act (1968)*], the appellant was plainly under an obligation to retain, if not the actual notes and coins, at least their proceeds, that is to say the money credited in the bank account which he opened for the trust with the actual property … Whether a person in the position of the appellant is a trustee is to be judged on an objective basis. It is an obligation imposed on him by law. It is not essential that he should have realised that he was a trustee …

APPROACH

9.16 These cases may often involve other parties – either independent fundraisers or more usually the activities of a trading company controlled by the charity in terms of shareholding. The investigation detail will come down to examining the financial aspects of the arrangements and also the question of the control which the trustees of the charity actually had over the activities of the other parties.

It can be expected that both the accounting and legal support teams of the Commissioners may become involved in such cases. There will also be some close working with the Inland Revenue on the activities of a trading subsidiary. Some of the specific investigation areas will centre on:

- fundraising methods;
- fundraising costs;
- fundraising relationships;

The growing use of professional fundraisers is a feature in all three of the areas highlighted and the choice of such fundraisers is obviously critical. Most are diligent, professional people who are good at what they do and bring considerable financial benefit to the charities for whom they work. Some are basically crooks who see charities as a soft touch and a means of earning easy money. For example, in a case highlighted in the 1991 Report of the Charity Commission, the promoter of a lottery associated with a charity had diverted 40% of the funds raised through the lottery to his own benefit. He and his associate were jailed for two years on charges including deception, false accounting, false information and illegally applying lottery proceeds.

The procedures for dealing with professional fundraisers have now been codified in the *Charities Act 1993* and there is much greater protection than in the past. It is still incumbent upon trustees to ensure that the arrangements they enter into are properly controlled and do not harm the charity in any way.

Fundraising methods

9.17 The Charity Commission, in their leaflet CC20 'Charities and fund-raising', makes it clear that the choice of methods of fundraising is one for trustees to decide upon. However (at para 4) it states:

> ... charities which are supported by donations need to be alert and sensitive to public opinion and criticism. Fund-raising methods which meet with disapproval can damage the charity and reduce public confidence in the sector as a whole.

This is obviously an area where the public issue will be important. If members of the public feel that fundraising methods are aggressive or intrusive they will object, and charities involved may find themselves involved in an enquiry and will have to justify their methods or change them. This applies whether the fundraising activities are carried out directly by the charity or by professional fundraisers acting on behalf of the charity.

The Commission will accept that charities are in a competitive situation when it comes to getting funds at all. The statistics show that people are giving proportionately less to charities now than a decade ago, and, in particular, young people are giving less. There is also competition between charities for the limited funds available. In a world that is more aggressive and 'in your face' than it was, charities or their fundraisers may feel that they have to adopt similar tactics to achieve justifiable charitable ends. The Charity Commission will need to be convinced. In the Charity Commission News 12 published in spring 2000, the Commissioners included a short article on 'Fundraising – manners make financial sense' and list suggestions received from funders and donors who had concerns about the ways in which they had been treated by fundraisers. The Commissioners point out that in a number of cases the people concerned had indicated that they would no longer be making donations to the particular charity.

One area that the Charity Commission is very keen to monitor is the control which a charity should maintain over those who fundraise on its behalf. This needs to include not only ensuring that funds are passed over, but also that the methods the fundraiser uses are not illegal in any way.

BABY ASSIST

9.18 A lack of control of fundraisers led to Baby Assist, a charity established to help premature babies, being wound up by the trustees. At the stage of registration, the Charity Commission had made recommendations about fundraising methods, but these were ignored by the trustees. A wide range of complaints was received from the public, supermarkets, local authorities and the police, which indicated that law and practice on making public collections was being flouted. Misleading information was being given to local authorities, some street collections were being conducted without any licence, and collections were being made on behalf of hospitals without their permission. The problem was compounded by the fact that the Commission could find no evidence that the funds raised were actually being used to support the charitable objects. Misleading information was given by the trustees about the handling of grant applications from hospitals. The fundraising activities had been entrusted to a community fundraiser appointed as an employee of the charity. No references were taken up and the employee was not asked about the methods he intended to use. He used other individuals who were under his control but not employees of the charity. The fundraiser and his staff all took commission from the collections. When the matter was brought to the attention of the trustees they dismissed the fundraiser, but problems continued and the trustees took the decision to wind up the charity.

BREAKAWAY TRUST

9.19 An enquiry, prompted by members of the public into the fundraising activities of a charity has led to that charity, Breakaway Trust, being closed and removed from the register. The fundraising was carried out under a fixed-term contract with a professional fundraiser and was based around the sale of a magazine. The problems arising were that the fundraiser continued to act after the agreement expired, they had not obtained the necessary permits because the magazine was predominantly sold door-to-door, and a member of the committee was said to have used the magazine to advertise his own business. In addition to these shortcomings, the Commissioners noted that the committee included members who were related to each other.

Control of non-charitable fundraising entities

9.20 The Charity Commission are always keen to stress that their jurisdiction operates over any situation in which funds are raised for charity even if those activities are run by a body which is not charitable. This will involve considering not only the methods used by the fundraisers but also the way in which they distribute the resulting funds.

FOXWOOD INTERNATIONAL LTD

9.21 Foxwood International Ltd was a commercial company which produced and sold a magazine, 'Sayit', which contained articles about local community and voluntary groups. The publicity indicated that each month a donation would be made to a charity of its readers' choosing. Complaints from the public indicated that sellers of the magazine were making claims that it was being sold on behalf of a charity. The owner of the company claimed he was unaware of these statements and was also unaware of the legal requirements of the *Charities Act 1992* on fundraising. The enquiry found that the allegations were substantiated and the company has now ceased to trade. The Charity Commission noted that it has used its powers under the *Charities Act 1993, s 10* to provide other interested regulatory bodies with details of the company's activities.

PEOPLE CARE NORTH WEST (PCNW)

9.22 People Care North West (PCNW) had been established as a charity, but following confirmation that it was, in reality, a fundraising operation, its charitable status was removed. The administrator continued to trade commercially using the PCNW name. The Commission received complaints about the activities including allegations that fundraising rules were not being followed and no proper control was being exercised. The Charity Commission liaised with local authorities and some charities on whose behalf funds had been raised. They found that PCNW was persistently failing to follow the Regulations. As a result of the enquiry, the activities of PCNW have been terminated although the Commission is maintaining a watching brief.

FA CHARITY SHIELD

9.23 Even prominent, regular fundraising events can have their problems. The Football Association (FA) Community Shield acts as a curtain-raiser to the football season each year and raises funds for a wide range of charities. The FA, which organises the event, is not itself a charity and when the Charity Commission looked into the ticket arrangements, the FA challenged its authority for so doing. The Commission maintained that once the funds from the gate money were received by the FA for distribution, that organisation became effectively charity trustees and fell under the aegis of the Commission. The problem with the tickets was that they gave no indication as to how the charitable element in the ticket price was to be calculated and distributed. The issue is to resolved by including details on the application form for tickets, pubishing details on the FA website and distributing details with the tickets.

Fundraising costs

9.24 A major area of Charity Commission concern will be in the costs of fundraising activities and ensuring that those costs are not excessive. It is not sufficient to argue that even a small part of the proceeds of a fundraising venture represent pure profit to the charity and huge expenses can therefore be justified. The Commission will accept that most fundraising ventures will incur costs of some kind – if only printing costs of leaflets or envelopes for a house-to-house collection. They will, however, expect that the costs will be kept to a minimum because that is what the public will also expect. The man in the street making his donation of £1 will expect that the charity will be able to use most of that £1 for the work it does – if he finds out that 50% or more of that donation has gone in expenses, he will believe that he has made his donation under false pretences and will rightly complain. Back in 1991, the Commissioners noted that in 19 cases they had investigated, the proportion of funds actually handed over to charities were less than 10%, and that they had acted to prevent further fundraising and had frozen the relevant accounts. Hopefully, the position is better after the enactment of the *Charities Act 1993*, but there are still cases of concern.

Charities under investigation in this area will need to be able to justify the level of expenses that have been incurred. In particular, they may need to justify the level of fees paid to external fundraisers. They may have to consider issues such as the following.

148

- Why was that method of fund-raising chosen if it was going to cost so much? There may be a justification in the extended publicity which an event generated which had a beneficial effect on donations in general.

- Were the costs of fundraising made clear in all the publicity? For example, was it made clear that celebrities involved were making a charge, or that only a proportion of royalties was going to the charity, or that the costs of the fund-raisers were a proportion of the proceeds?

- Were the costs of using external fundraisers lower than the costs of recruiting and employing people in a fundraising department?

Two particular cases which appeared in the list of enquiry cases in 2001 illustrate some of the problems in keeping costs in perspective and in recognising that fundraising should always be a means to an end and not an end in itself. These cases involved the Foundation for Nephrology and World Villages for Children (see **9.25** and **9.26** below).

FOUNDATION FOR NEPHROLOGY

9.25 The costs of fundraising were a major issue in the investigation into the Foundation for Nephrology, a charity established to relieve people suffering from kidney disease. The enquiry was a lengthy one, having started in 1997, and is worth looking at in some detail. A company, Medical Aid (UK) Ltd, was used to conduct the fundraising activities on behalf of the charity. This company was controlled by the Executive Chairman and the Financial Controller of the charity. The company shared office premises and staff with the charity but no clear distinction was made in allocating costs. The Charity Commission found that in four years from February 1996, Medical Aid collected almost £5million from the public but paid only £260,000 to the charity. In one year, nothing at all was paid over. Included in the funds were cash donations from the public which should have been paid directly to the charity.

The trustees, who were all respected medical professionals, did decide how to spend the money but they relied totally on the two individuals involved with the charity and company to handle that relationship. The trustees never met the auditors and were found to have exercised little or no control over fundraising expenditure. The two individuals were clearly in a position where they had interests in both bodies and it was entirely inappropriate for them to have acted in the way they did.

The findings of the enquiry showed that only 10% of the £7million raised from the public had actually been used for charitable purposes and that payments and benefits to the management team and their family were regularly in excess of the charitable activity.

The Commission's concerns were put to the trustees who appear to have failed to address the real issue of the low rate of return. They conceded that they did not have the financial expertise to review the position and welcomed the appointment of a receiver and manager. The receiver concluded that the

fundraising operation could not be justified on cost grounds but in the absence
of any other sources of funds the charity should be wound up.

WORLD VILLAGES FOR CHILDREN

9.26   There is a real danger for many charities that fundraising can become an end in
itself rather than a means to an end in providing funds to allow the charitable
objects to take place. That was the conclusion the Charity Commission came
to in its investigation into the World Villages for Children. On the trustees'
own projections, the percentage of fundraising costs to fundraising income was
going to reduce from 65% to 56% over a five-year period and the Commission
considered that this was too high. In addition, they were unhappy that certain
printed matter, which the charity argued was furthering the objects, was in
reality simply fundraising material. The level of complaints which had been
received about fundraising practices was damaging the reputation of the charity and putting the property of the charity at risk. The charity agreed to review
its fundraising activities on a regular basis to ensure that it was effective, economic and responsive to the cultural context in which the charity operates.

Fundraising relationships

9.27   The *Charities Act 1993* sets out the legal framework for relationships between
charities and professional fundraisers. It covers the following areas:

- legally enforceable agreements to cover fundraising;

- disclosure of beneficiaries and remuneration;

- repayment of donations made;

- the right of charities to prevent unauthorised fundraising;

- penalties for making false statements.

The legislation applies to agreements between charities and professional
fundraisers, and also to agreements between charities and other organisations
referred to as 'commercial participators'. This covers, in particular, the relationship between charities and commercial sponsors.

The Commissioners would expect now that any link with a professional
fundraiser was governed by an agreement which complied with the *Charities
Act 1993* and any charity which had failed to do this would be in serious trou-
ble.

There are also signs that the Commissioners are becoming increasingly concerned that some relationships between charities and companies, whilst finan-
cially very attractive, may be putting charity assets at risk. In particular, they
are concerned about the use of the charity name by the commercial concern.
They state in leaflet CC20 at para 43:

> A charity's name is precious. It is the means by which the charity is known
> and by which its reputation will be judged. We strongly recommend that

trustees be careful how they allow it to be used, especially by a commercial participator during a promotional venture.

The exploitation of a charity logo, many of which are very distinctive and well-known would fall into the same category.

Charities under investigation in this area will need to provide evidence to show that they have not harmed themselves by particular associations. This may actually prove to be very difficult and they will find themselves under some pressure to change arrangements.

DIAL-A-DREAM

9.28 Charities want to demonstrate to donors that they run tight operations and that funds go primarily to the objects of the charity. Finding the right words for this can be difficult as Dial-a-Dream, a charity set up to provide holidays for terminally ill children discovered. Its fundraising literature proclaimed that 'every penny goes to the children', a claim that simply could not be backed up by a review of its accounts. The charity had wanted to explain that it did not pay any wages as it was staffed by volunteers and did not maintain an office to keep costs down. It accepted that it needed to use alternative wording.

PROMILLA JERATH CHILDREN'S TRUST

9.29 The enquiry into the Promilla Jerath Children's Trust was a follow up to a previous enquiry which centred on the activities of rose sellers who operated through a commercial company called 'Thoughts Postal Flowers'. The Charity Commission had concluded the inquiry on the basis that the trustees would decide on one of three options to take to put the fundraising on to a proper legal basis. Continued complaints about the activities of the rose sellers prompted the further enquiry. The trustees told the Commission that they were putting a formal agreement into place, but the Commission told them that they must cease all involvement immediately until an agreement was reached. In the event, no agreement could be reached and the trustees decided to wind up the charity.

SUNDERLAND PACE

9.30 The enquiry into Sunderland PACE focused on the activities of commercial fundraisers. They operated under a formal agreement but it became clear that some work was done by individuals who were paid a commission and engaged in a self-employed capacity. Each of these should have had their own agreement with the charity.

WILDFOWL AND WETLANDS TRUST

9.31 It is important to ensure that, where arrangements are in place with a commercial participator under which donations are to be made in respect of purchases made, the publicity should be clear both as to the basis of donation and the charity involved. In the investigation into Wildfowl and Wetlands Trust, the Charity Commission found that arrangements with wine merchants were simply too vague and gave only the acronym WWT. Both the charity and the commercial operator agreed to spell out the precise basis of donations and to show the full name of the charity.

Inland Revenue investigations

Introduction

9.32 In the context of tax efficient giving, the major approach of the Inland Revenue is in the use of audit visits to charities to inspect records which are the key components of the Gift Aid audit trail. Specific legislation which grants the right of enquiry in the case of a charity pre-dated the self-assessment regime and is found in the *Finance (No 2) Act 1992, s 28*. This states that where a charity, or other body which can seek exemption under either *ICTA 1988, s 507* or *s 508*, has made such a claim, and the claim results in the repayment (actual or potential) of income tax or a payment of tax credit then:

> The Board may require the body to produce for inspection by an officer of the Board all such books, documents and other records in the possession of or under the control, of the body as contain information relating to the claim.

The power can be used not only against a charity but also against a heritage body and also a body engaged in scientific research.

The power to require the production of basic records is formidable. It is not, for example, open as a matter of course in investigations into traders, although a similar power exists in the area of PAYE investigations. There is no requirement that it should be used only in cases in which the Inland Revenue believes that an excessive claim may have been made. The power is seen by the Inland Revenue as a key part of its policy of 'pay now, examine later' which has allowed them to speed up the processing of repayment claims made by charities. It is the price that charities have to pay for that service.

The power as it stands in the legislation is, however, only one of inspection of books of account, documents and other written records. It does not allow the Inland Revenue to ask any questions it likes about the charity's affairs. There are other powers that can be used to elicit information from either the taxpayer or a third party and it should not be assumed that charities are outside the scope of such legislation.

Repayment checks

SELECTION PROCESS

9.33 The repayment section has to handle just under 200,000 repayment claims a year from over 40,000 charities. Many of these charities are small, and for many excepted charities, the repayment of tax in respect of Gift Aid and deeds of covenant, is their only exposure to the regulatory regime.

A decade ago, the process was long and tedious with each claim being checked and a range of background information having to be submitted. For example, all deeds of covenant had to be sent in, and all Gift Aid Certificates had to be submitted. Charities could wait several months for a repayment. Now the process is one of 'repay now, check later' and the aim is to pay 95% of claims within ten days of receipt. The range of information which has to be submitted has also been substantially reduced, and is being reduced still further under the new Gift Aid procedures. Basically, no additional documentation will now be required with the claim form which will list the total being reclaimed.

The repayment claims are checked against the list of charities on the databases to ensure that they are from bodies which qualify for charitable exemption. Larger claims are subject to arithmetical checks. The claims details are passed through a computer which provides an analysis based on a points system, which includes changes in the charity since the last claim and the size of the claim but not any risk associated with the compliance history of the charity.

Information available suggests that three categories of claim are submitted for a more detailed check to ensure that they meet legal requirements and that any supporting documentation matches up. Those three groups are:

● all first claims;

● all claims over a certain (unspecified) amount;

● a small sample of other claims.

As far as the charity is concerned, any amendment to their claim will be dealt with in writing and, in most cases, there will be no further action taken.

TAX TO COVER CHECKS

9.34 One important part of the repayment process is that of ensuring that donors have paid sufficient tax on their own income to cover the tax being reclaimed by the charity. This is referred to as 'tax to cover'. Again, as part of the streamlining process (and also as a reflection of the improved tracing procedures in the Inland Revenue), very little information is now required about the donor. The new arrangements will require only the donor's name and address.

Inland Revenue (Charity) send out details to local districts of all Gift Aid claims over a specified (but unnamed) level and ask for notification if insufficient tax has been paid. The job of dealing with the unpaid tax in these cases falls on to the local districts dealing with the donors. It is the donor who must make good any deficiency and Inland Revenue (Charity) will always repay the charity. In one situation these checks uncovered systematic abuse of the system by a group of charities that involved potential losses in excess of £2million and that these were reviewed by the Revenue Special Compliance Office.

Audits

SELECTION PROCESS

9.35 The use of audits is aimed at monitoring the validity of claims to repayment in respect of Gift Aid. Essentially, the reviews are going to focus on the documentation and audit trail and on the question of donor benefit, which were discussed in detail in **Chapter 2** and **Chapter 4**.

Prior to 1997, Inland Revenue (Charity) selected audit cases on the basis of a minimum annual claim of £5,000 and auditor judgment. A review of the operation of Inland Revenue (Charity) by the National Audit Office (NAO) identified one church with annual repayment claims of over £100,000 which had never had an audit. It also pointed out that 20% of the 6,400 charities making the largest claims had never had an audit.

The Inland Revenue has now introduced a risk-targeting system which concentrates resources on the larger claims. The largest 6,400 are to be audited on a three- to ten-year cycle – the frequency of visits being dependent upon an assessment of risk built up from:

- whether there has been a previous audit;
- the size of the annual repayment claim;
- the size of claim in respect of investment income;
- previous audit history;
- charity type.

The remaining 40,000 plus charities which make claims are to be audited on a sample basis.

APPROACH – SINGLE SITES

9.36 The basic audit approach is to:

- carry out a visit to the charity;
- prepare a report to the charity within six weeks;
- agree a settlement if that is appropriate.

Before a visit takes place there will be some preparatory work, usually reviewing the claims history and, in the case of non-church charities, having a review of the charity's most recent accounts undertaken by an accounts inspector. The NAO note that this latter practice yields 'productive results'.

The visit has been replaced by a desk-based audit for very small charities because this is considered to be a more productive use of time by the auditor. The average total time for a desk-based audit is stated to be five hours as against 13 hours for the full audit.

The visit to the charity will, in many cases, be to the home of the treasurer (certainly in the case of church cases). The visit can take up to a day depending on how many individual items there are and how good the record-keeping is. Essentially, the auditor is looking for an audit trail to establish that the sums received came from the particular donor. Documentation and evidence are the key, particularly where cash receipts are concerned. The question of donor benefit will also be a significant area of interest.

The auditor will expect to deal with most items in the course of the visit and will discuss any problems at the time. He will prepare a report which will set out the extent of the review and will detail all the items which are wrong and quantify the errors. One thing that he will seek to establish is whether the errors are peculiar to the year reviewed or whether they should be seen as symptoms of a wider problem. He may decide to extend his review to an earlier year and then decided if a wider approach is needed.

The negotiation of a settlement will usually involve a repayment of the tax overclaimed, it will probably involve interest and may also include a penalty element – depending on the view that the auditor takes of why the problem has arisen.

APPROACH – MULTIPLE SITES

9.37 There are situations where substantial claims are made on behalf of a number of different claimants by a central body. For example, a diocese may make a claim on behalf of all the constituent churches. This saves local treasurers the task of making claims and also reduces substantially the number of individual claims received by the Inland Revenue. The Inland Revenue audit approach in these cases is to take a sample of cases and review the records for these. Errors found are noted and an overall error rate is calculated which is then extrapolated across the total population for the year of review and earlier years as well.

In one case seen by the author, the Inland Revenue took a sample of 15 churches from a population of 400. It found an overall error rate which it initially set at 1.29% and extrapolated this across the full sample for six years.

Negotiating on single site audits

9.38 Where the Inland Revenue (Charity) audit looks at a single charity, it will be a matter for the trustees of that charity to negotiate a settlement with the Inland Revenue. The actual review may have taken account of just one year but the Inland Revenue may seek to use it to go back over a number of years and to review the repayment claims made. There are two areas for arguing in this case.

155

- First and foremost argue as to why particular payments should be allowed. Obviously this will depend upon the facts and the evidence available. Look carefully at the arguments that are being advanced and see how they might be rebutted. Issues relating to the audit trail and identification may be provable in other ways. It may be possible to reduce the potential value of benefits below the limit in the legislation or indeed to argue that there is no benefit at all.

- The second stage is to consider the carry back of the consequences of the first year. This should be relatively easy in the first few years of the new Gift Aid scheme because it is likely that there would not have been the level of Gift Aid donations in earlier years. This may remain an argument once the scheme moves forward. The other significant argument will always be that the issues found in the first year are peculiar to that year and would be unlikely to have been found in earlier years. This may be the case, for example, with particular benefits received by some donors because the benefit was not available in the earlier years. The aim is to minimise the potential base that is being used for the carry-back calculation.

EXAMPLE 9.1

The Inland Revenue visits a church for an audit in 2005. The total tax reclaims in the last tax year 2004/05 amounted to £13,500. The auditor reviews all of these and finds some irregularities. These include:

- a donation of £500 (tax £140) made to support a church member going to Bible College. The donation, however, came from the individual's sister and should not qualify under the benefit rules;

- three donations where repayment was claimed but there is no evidence in the church accounts that enables the donor to be identified. The tax on these totals £800.

The auditor decides that on the basis of his review he wants £940 back from the church for 2004/05. He also decides that as the error rate is 7% (£940 on £13,500), he is going to require repayment of a similar percentage of the tax repaid on claims for 2000/01, and subsequent years. The tax repaid in those four years totalled £40,000 and the auditor is looking for a settlement of £2,800 plus the £940.

The treasurer cannot argue about the benefit point for 2004/05 but he does make the point that there is clear evidence to show that there were no payments of a similar nature made in earlier years because the student in question only went to college in that year and no other student has been supported in a similar way. Of the other three payments he manages to find evidence in the books of one of the payments because the donor is able to identify the precise date on which they made the payment by information from their own bank details. This is for tax of £280.

The impact of these adjustments is that the tax due for 2004/05 becomes only £660 and the sum to be used for extrapolation is only £520 or 3.8%. This reduces the reclaim for earlier years to £1,520.

Negotiating on multiple sites

9.39 It was noted at **9.37** above that the Inland Revenue has adopted a policy in some cases of dealing with audits on a sample basis. These are situations where one body, possibly a diocese, makes repayment claims on behalf of some, or all, of the churches in the diocese. This saves the individual churches making the claims and also reduces the number of claims the Inland Revenue has to check through the repayment process. The audit approach which the Inland Revenue likes to agree is that it will visit a sample of churches and then want to extrapolate the results of the sample, not only down the years as in the example above, but also across the whole sample. There is no statutory basis for this – it is simply saving the Inland Revenue time and money but it could be an approach that is very expensive for the claim-making charity. The charity should actually consider very carefully if it is willing to accept this approach because, as the example below shows, it can have significant impact on the central organisation and also possibly on charities that have been impeccable in their compliance.

The basic Inland Revenue view is that if the sample is reasonable, then errors found can reasonably be extrapolated. This ignores basic rules of sampling error and makes the sweeping assumption that the same types of mistake must have been made across the sample. This may be true when looking at a machine process which might make errors but, in this case, the consideration is for very individual claims recorded by a significant number of individual treasurers all of whom are aware of the system.

It is the author's view that charities in this situation should think very carefully before they agree to a sample approach like this. If the Inland Revenue is not prepared to visit all the locations included in the claim, then any extrapolation should be limited to the venues covered in the sample and not the whole population. After all, that would be the situation if each charity was visited individually.

Consider this example which is based on an actual case (the names have been changed to protect the innocent).

Barchester Diocese submitted a repayment claim on behalf of some 400 churches in the diocese. The claims made each year were as follows:

1999/00	£1,498,356
2000/01	£1,490,702
2001/02	£1,445,940
2002/03	£1,359,031
2003/04	£1,295,773
2004/05	£1,327,084

The Inland Revenue decided to sample check the claim for 2004/05. It was agreed by someone representing the diocese that 15 churches should be visited and that an extrapolated result would be obtained. The visits took place and the auditors report was received. This showed the following results.

157

Church	Claim	Errors	IR percentage
Church 1	£23,266	0	0.00
Church 2	£11,666	0	0.00
Church 3	£8,042	574	7.14
Church 4	£15,474	92	0.59
Church 5	£9,628	201	2.09
Church 6	£15,167	369	2.43
Church 7	£31,398	189	0.60
Church 8	£12,968	0	0.00
Church 9	£5,749	98	1.71
Church 10	£4,732	457	3.10
Church 11	£953	0	0.00
Church 12	£13,486	222	1.65
Church 13	£9,075	0	0.00
Church 14	£12,224	219	1.79
Church 15	£8,647	157	1.82
Total	**£201,475**	**2,578**	**1.53**

On the basis of this sample, the repayments for earlier years were to be reclaimed to the extent of 1.53%, which meant a total repayment of £127,937.

The first point to note is that the Inland Revenue percentage of 1.53% is the average percentage in the cases where errors were found. If the total value of errors is taken as a percentage of the total gross reclaim from the sample churches, then the real error rate drops to 1.28% and the claim by the Inland Revenue falls to £107,736 – a drop of £20,000 which is more than significant. The Inland Revenue argued the validity for its original percentage but conceded the lower point after discussion. If a sample is to be used, the results must be based on the whole sample, not just the 'guilty' part of the sample.

Subsequent close scrutiny of the errors and some extra work by the centre has enabled the Inland Revenue to agree that the revised total error figure should be only £1,892, a percentage of 0.94%, making the total claim now £79,118.

Overall, the negotiations have reduced the Inland Revenue claim by almost £50,000, but there remains a significant problem for the centre. They have to find the tax – do they take this out of some central fund or do they seek redress from all the churches for whom they made the return? Spread over all 400 churches, the cost would be £200 per church, but some churches who were not in the sample (and those that were shown by the sample to be all clear) could justifiably say that they had no liability. Why should they pay up for what is a statistical not a proven charge?

Moving to a settlement

FINALISING THE TAX

9.40 In audit cases, as we have seen at **9.37** above, the usual approach from the Inland Revenue is to go back over a six-year period, assuming, of course, that repayment claims have been made throughout that period. The Inland Revenue's right to do so stems from its legal right to raise assessments within what is known as the ordinary time period. For accounting periods up to June 1999, the ordinary time limit was six years of assessment, now the limit is expressed as:

> ... any time not later than five years after the 31st January next following the year of assessment to which it relates.

So, for a reclaim relating to 2003/04, the ordinary time limit will run to five years from 31 January 2005 and will, therefore, expire on 31 January 2010. Under the old rules the time limit for 2003/04 would have run to 5 April 2010.

The time limit is extended where there is fraudulent or negligent conduct by the *Taxes Management Act 1970, s 36*:

> An assessment on any person (in this section referred to as 'the person in default') for the purpose of making good to the Crown a loss of income tax or capital gains tax attributable to his fraudulent or negligent conduct or the fraudulent or negligent conduct of a person acting on his behalf may be made at any time not later than 20 years after the 31st January next following the year of assessment to which it relates.

This does, of course, mean that arguments about whether the charity is guilty of fraudulent or negligent conduct become significant if the Inland Revenue is seeking to go back more than six years.

INTEREST

9.41 The Inland Revenue is entitled to charge interest on any tax which is not paid at the correct time. The interest will run from the date on which the tax should have been paid. In the case of tax over-repaid, the interest will usually run from the date on which the incorrect repayment was made.

DEALING WITH PENALTIES

9.42 The Inland Revenue is able to charge penalties where tax has been lost due to fraudulent or negligent conduct. Where mistakes have been made in repayment claims because of inefficiencies in the audit trail or because of benefit issues relating to the donor, the Inland Revenue is going to argue that neglect has occurred. If a charity was caught having made clearly false repayment claims they could expect the Inland Revenue to take a very serious view of the position.

9.43   Keeping the Regulators Happy

The Inland Revenue will calculate the maximum penalty as the total amount of tax lost as a result of the offence. It then mitigates that penalty by taking account of three broad areas as follows.

- The extent of disclosure made by the taxpayer can influence up to 20% of the penalty. If the charity knows that there are mistakes, an early disclosure of those errors – certainly before the Inland Revenue begins its review – will gain the maximum abatement in this area.

- The level of co-operation by the taxpayer affects up to 40% of the penalty. Co-operation does not mean an absence of argument, but it is affected by factors such as the speed of response to correspondence.

- The final area is the size and gravity of the offence. If fraud is involved, the abatement will be very small. Where it is a simple error, the abatement should be near the maximum of 40%.

Letter of offer

9.43 In most cases where interest and penalties are involved, the Inland Revenue will look to resolve the case by means of a letter of offer because this will save the paperwork of raising assessments for each year.

Appendix

Charity Repayment Claim

 Inland **Revenue**

The box below is for Inland Revenue use only		*Please complete if the Reference, Charity name and Address boxes are blank.*
Date claim received	/ /	Reference
Claim sub no.		Charity name
Arith. check Initials	Date / /	Address
Authorised Initials	Date / /	
√ *if appropriate* Notification ☐ Advice ☐		

Please

- **Read R68(Notes)** before completing this claim.
- Use *CAPITAL LETTERS* when filling out this form and √ boxes as appropriate.
- Tell us immediately if the charity's name changes or if you are a new signatory. Don't wait until you claim repayment as any change may cause delay.
- Make a copy of the claim or schedules if you need to before sending them in.
- Don't send correspondence unless it relates to the claim.
- When you have finished fold this form in half and use the return envelope provided.
- Make sure that the address, to which you are returning the form, is clearly visible in the envelope window.

Part 1   Amount of repayment claim

In respect of each source of income below

- complete the appropriate schedule, **and**
- enter the tax/relief claimed.

Tax/relief claimed

1. **Other income received under deduction of tax.**
   Enter the total amount of tax deducted - Schedule R68(F).

   1 £

2. **New Gift Aid**
   Enter the total amount of tax claimed from Schedule R68 (New Gift Aid)

   2 £

3. **Transitional relief on distributions paid on or after 6 April 1999.**
   Enter the total relief claimed - Schedule R68(TCTR).

   3 £

   add boxes 1,2, and 3

4. **Total tax/relief claimed.**

   4 £

5. **Sponsored Events**
   Has the charity included donations received from Sponsored fundraising event(s) in this claim? For example, Sponsored Walks, Marathons, Cycle Rides

   √ *as appropriate*

   Yes ☐   No ☐

R68(2000) **(Substitute)(LexisNexis)**

Appendix

Part 2 Charity details

1 Is the charity's name as shown overleaf?

Yes ☐ No ☐

If 'No', please enter the correct name of the charity below and send a copy of the document confirming the change of name.

2 Is the charity a company for tax purposes?
(See note 5)

Yes ☐ No ☐

If 'Yes' please enter the date the accounts period ends *(See note 6)*

Day ☐ Month ☐

All repayments are now dealt with in our Bootle office. Please send all completed forms to the address printed opposite. If you have any questions about the repayment process please call **08453 02 02 03.**

Inland Revenue Charities
Repayments (Code 361A)
St John's House
Merton Road
Bootle, Merseyside
L69 9BB

Part 3 Repayment details

1 Period to which the claim relates.

From ☐ / /

To ☐ / /

Building Society reference number ☐

Account number ☐

Branch sort code ☐ — —

2 Where is the repayment to be sent?
Tick one of the following boxes

• direct to your bank or building society ☐

• to a nominee ☐

• by cheque to the address shown overleaf ☐

• by cheque to a different address ☐

3 Fill in this section if the repayment is to be sent to your, or your nominee's, bank or building society account

Name of bank or building society

Name of account for use by BACS
(first 28 characters including spaces)

4 Authorisation - fill in this section if the repayment is to be sent to a nominee or to a different address.

Nominee's name and reference *(if appropriate)*

Nominee's address

Name and address to which cheque should be sent

Name and address for acknowledgement to be sent

Signature of an authorised officer of the charity

Part 4 Declaration

An authorised official of the charity must complete and sign the Declaration

1 Title ☐ Full name

2 Your official position, for example, Treasurer, Secretary, Trustee. ☐

3 Phone number at which we may contact you if we have a question about this claim. ☐

I claim the sum of £ ☐ as shown in box 4 overleaf

I declare to the best of my knowledge and belief:
• the information given on this form is correct and complete and
• the charity is exempt from tax under Sections 505, 507 or 508 ICTA 1988 in respect of the income shown on this form.

I understand that false statements can lead to prosecution.

Signed ☐ Date / /

162

Schedule to Charity Repayment Claim

Inland
Revenue
IR Charities

Reference

Please use a separate schedule for each tax
year and ensure that you enter the charity's tax
reference in the box above on all schedules.

Sheet number

For claims from 6 April _____ to 5 April _____
(Enter year)   *(Enter year)*

Schedule of New Gift Aid donations made by individuals

Do NOT send declarations with this claim

- Use this schedule to record donations made on or after 6 April 2000 by individuals. The basic rate of tax for the years 6/4/2000 to 5/4/2002 is 22%.

- This schedule must be accompanied by form R68(2000). Please complete all columns to avoid delay and possible restriction of claim.

- Ensure that for each payment or series of payments included in this claim, the donor has made a declaration that the payment(s) are to be made tax effective.

- Where a series of payments from the same donor are to be included in this claim enter the **total** donations for the above tax year and the date of the **last** payment in the series.

- If you do not have enough space on the schedule make a photocopy or attach a separate sheet. Enter the total tax claimed at Box 2 on form R68(2000).

Name of donor	Date of payment or last payment in series	Total donation(s) received
Brought forward from previous schedule *(if applicable)*		£
1.		£
2.		£
3.		£
4.		£
5.		£
6.		£
7.		£
8.		£
9.		£
10.		£
11.		£
12.		£
13.		£
14.		£
15.		£
16.		£
17.		£
Total carried forward overleaf		£

R68(New Gift Aid) **(Substitute)(LexisNexis)**

Appendix

Name of donor	Date of payment or last payment in series	Total donation(s) received	
Carried forward from previous page		£	
18.		£	
19.		£	
20.		£	
21.		£	
22.		£	
23.		£	
24.		£	
25.		£	
26.		£	
27.		£	
28.		£	
29.		£	
30.		£	
31.		£	
32.		£	
33.		£	
34.		£	
35.		£	
36.		£	
37.		£	
38.		£	
39.		£	
40.		£	
41.		£	
42.		£	
43.		£	
44.		£	
45.		£	
46.		£	
Total donations received *(carried forward to next schedule if appropriate)* **A**		£	

Total tax claimed = A x $^{22}/_{78}$ *(transfer to box 2 on form R68(2000))* £

Index

165

Index

Index

Index

Index

Index